AMERICAN SIGN LANGUAGE:
A BEGINNING COURSE

CATHERINE KETTRICK

ILLUSTRATIONS BY PAUL M. SETZER

A Publication of

The National Association of The Deaf
814 Thayer Avenue • Silver Spring, Maryland 20910

AMERICAN SIGN LANGUAGE: A BEGINNING COURSE

CATHERINE KETTRICK

Copyright © 1984 by Catherine Kettrick

Published by the National Association of the Deaf

ISBN 0-913072-64-8

Printed in the United States of America

To My Parents

ACKNOWLEDGEMENTS

Now that I'm writing a page of acknowledgements instead of reading one, I realize that all of the cliches are true: there are many people Without Whom This Book Would Not Have Been Possible and they are all Far Too Numerous To Mention. Nevertheless I do want to mention several people to whom I am deeply indebted. Thanks are due to:

three members of the Department of Foreign Languages at Seattle University, *Sr. Clarence Abello, M. R. Maxime Marononi* and *M. Paul Milan,* whose method of teaching served as a model for this text and whose own understanding and love of teaching showed me how much fun it can be to learn another language;

Eric Malzkuhn, from whom I first started learning what was then "sign language" and whose casual comments about interpreting one afternoon eventually led me into this field;

Theresa Smith, my "boss", for taking a chance on a new teacher with a different method of teaching;

all the people Deaf and Hearing, from whom I'm learning ASL and whom I pestered unmercifully for grammaticality judgements;

my many students, who suffered with xeroxed copies of endless versions of the student text and were the unwitting Guinea pigs for all my new ideas;

Marina McIntire, for reviewing the texts and for her helpful suggestions and support;

Mark Hoshi, for his time and valuable suggestions in helping me proof the manuscript;

Eugene Orr from the Guild, Inc. for his patience and willingness to undertake the difficult lay-out design project this has been;

Paul Setzer, for his incredible patience in drawing, drawing and re-drawing all the illustrations;

Mel Carter, Jr., for his guidance, support and enormous help in making it Really Happen;

and lastly, thanks to all my friends who don't even know they helped, but whose love and encouragement was invaluable.

About the Models

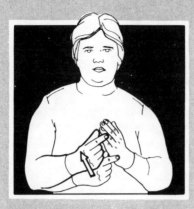

CAROL MONIGAN

Deaf from birth
Deaf Parents
Mother, with four Deaf Children ranging
from 12 to 17 years old
Mail Clerk

TRACI SHANNON LEGLER

Deaf from birth
Daughter of Deaf Parents
Student at School for the Deaf

DON LEITCH

Deaf from birth
Son of Deaf Parents and Grandparents
Two Deaf Sisters, and Deaf Relatives
Deaf Wife and three Hearing Daughters
Consultant

NORMAN INGRAM

Deaf from birth
Son of Deaf Father, Hearing Mother
Six Deaf Brothers and Sisters
Maintenance Engineer

INTRODUCTION

There are many reasons people sign up for a class in a foreign or second language. Some people are only interested in "survival" language—phrases useful while travelling or for minimum contact with people in another country. Some people are only interested in acquiring competence in reading the language. For these two groups courses focusing on specific vocabulary and specific phrases are often quite appropriate, and an appropriate method to teach the language for these courses might be to translate between the students' native language and the language being studied. But for people who are interested in learning to communicate fluently on all levels in the new language and who are interested in the culture of the people who use that language a different approach must be used. This text is designed for students in this last category, students who wish to learn ASL so that they can communicate fluently using it, and who also want to learn something about the culture of Deaf people.

The first thing you might notice if you casually flip through this book is that there are no English words with any of the pictures of signs. English captions were left out because the text is designed for classes where ASL is taught without translating. This means that the teacher will not use voice while signing, and any English that is used in the classroom will probably be in a written form. If this idea seems strange to you, consider how you learned your native language. From the time you were born you heard or saw native users of that language and gradually you began to understand it. No one translated for you—you had no other language to translate into—but by observing, watching, listening and using your innate capacity for learning languages you began to learn meanings of words and to figure out grammatical rules so that by the time you started school you knew the basics of your first language. You also learned a lot about the culture in which you lived because to know a language from the inside out is to begin to know the culture of which that language is a part.

Now as an adult you don't want to take five or six years to learn ASL as a child would, simply by being exposed to it. Furthermore, you already know at least one language and its rules, and might be inclined to learn a second more quickly if its rules are explained to you, rather than you trying to deduce them on your own by trial and error. On the other hand, simply telling you what different signs mean out of context, and in no particular order, and explaining rules without giving you the benefit of seeing them in operation would not be much help either. So, this text is designed to offer what may be the best of both worlds. There are no translations provided for the signs, so your teacher can present them without giving you a meaning in English, which will allow you to use your intuition to figure out the meanings for yourself. To make the process easier, the signs taught first will be those for concrete things in the environment (e.g., chair, table, window, woman, man, etc.) and for simple concepts (e.g., what, have, give, mine, who). As you learn these signs, gradually the lessons will become more abstract and complex. Each lesson will build on what went before in a natural progression. New concepts will be introduced either through pictures, drawings, props, mime or gestures, or by using signs already learned.

By now you may have realized that you as a student have a great responsibility. Namely, you have to understand each lesson before going on to the next, because if there are signs you don't understand, and those signs are used to teach new concepts, you won't be able to learn the new concepts either. So if there is something you are unsure about, you must ask, either using what ASL you have already learned, or with gestures, or in writing. And by going through this process of figuring out meanings for yourself, you will find that you become much more directly involved in the class, the class will be more enjoyable, and best of all, when you do understand something, you will remember it for a much longer time than if someone had merely translated for you.

The book is divided into 19 lessons, each of which has vocabulary items, and any grammatical and cultural information to be presented along with that lesson. The vocabulary is presented either with a picture of the object that a sign stands for, or in the context of a definition, using signs that you already know. Ideally a student text would include the stories and dialogues presented in class, with the vocabulary in the context of those stories, but ASL does not have a written form and space will not permit including the amount of information necessary to the student in the form of pictures of signs. Static pictures are not adequate representations of the language in any case, and the vocabulary is presented this way only as an aid in helping you remember the signs you learned during class.

The grammatical and cultural information that goes along with each lesson is presented in written English, because of the reasons given above and also because at the beginning of the course you do not have enough vocabulary to permit a full explanation in ASL alone. In addition, reading the information in English before class will aid your understanding of the teacher's presentation. By the latter part of the course you will have become accustomed to receiving information visually, rather than using your hearing, will be able to distinguish differences between signs and learn their meanings faster, and be able to acquire more information in ASL.

Although it is important that eventually you learn to sign clearly and easily, it is far more important for this class that you learn to *understand* what you are seeing. Children understand language before they express themselves using it, and any of you who have acquired a second aural/oral language probably have noticed that your understanding of the language was greater than your ability to speak it. With ASL there is the additional factor that you will be expressing yourself gesturally rather than vocally and it may take you more time to become accustomed to using your hands, face and whole body as a means of expression, instead of relying mostly on your voice.

ASL is a rich and complex language, different in some ways from aural/oral languages and similar in some ways. It will probably be as difficult to learn as any other foreign language. But it will also be as easy. Have fun.

CONTENTS

Introduction

GRAMMAR

Sentence Structure

This lesson introduces four sentence patterns that occur in ASL: wh questions, yes/no questions, simple declarative sentences, and simple negated sentences.

Questions

Wh questions are called that because wh-words occur in them (who, what, when, how many, how, why, where, etc). They cannot be answered by saying yes or no. Yes/no questions on the other hand do need a yes or no answer, although the person answering may go on to give more information.

English can use different voice inflections to distinguish between these two sentence types; ASL uses a different non-manual signal for each. Look at the pictures below:

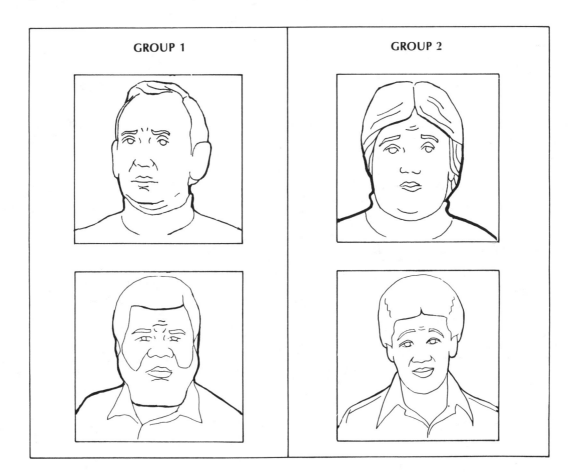

Can you see differences in the facial expressions between the two groups? The pictures in Group 1 show the non-manual grammatical signal used in ASL to mark wh questions; Group 2, the non-manual grammatical signal used to mark yes/no questions.

2

 Grammar - AMERICAN SIGN LANGUAGE:

Negation and Assertion

Although ASL has signs for the English equivalent of "yes," "no" and "not," a non-manual signal usually accompanies the sign or sentence being asserted or negated. These signals are similar to ones used in English when shaking your head no or nodding yes. Sometimes with simple sentences or with parts of more complex sentences, the non-manual signal is used without the sign. Here are some examples:

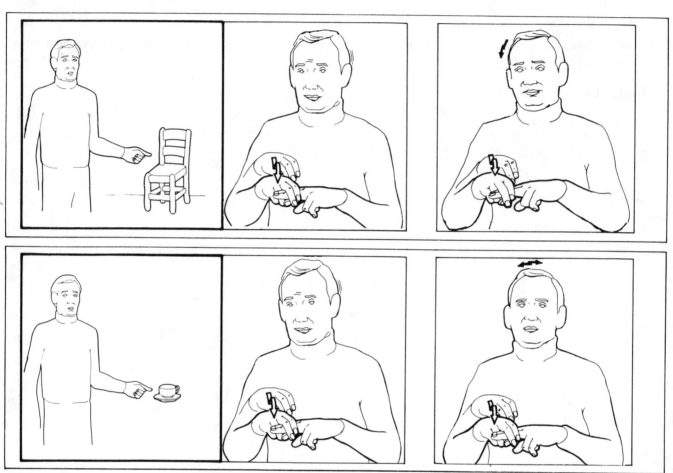

Practice asking and answering both wh and yes/no questions using the vocabulary from this lesson. Here are some examples for models:

Question

Answer

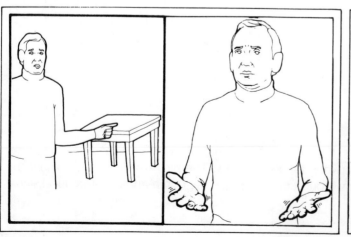
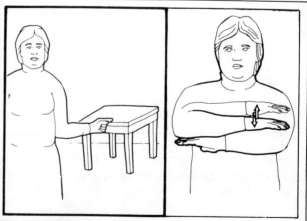

Question:

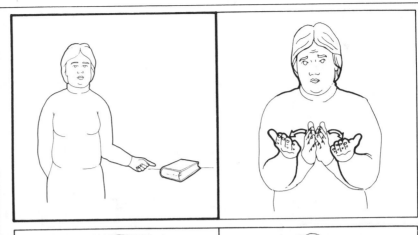

Answer:

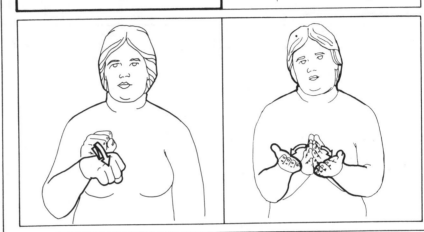

Question:

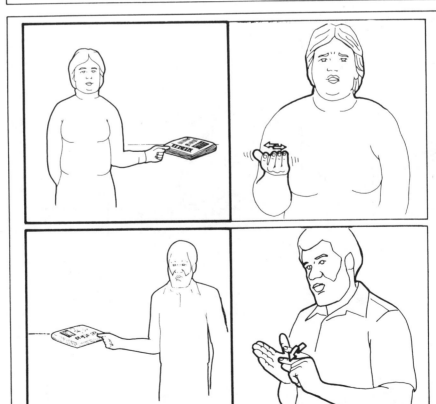

Answer:

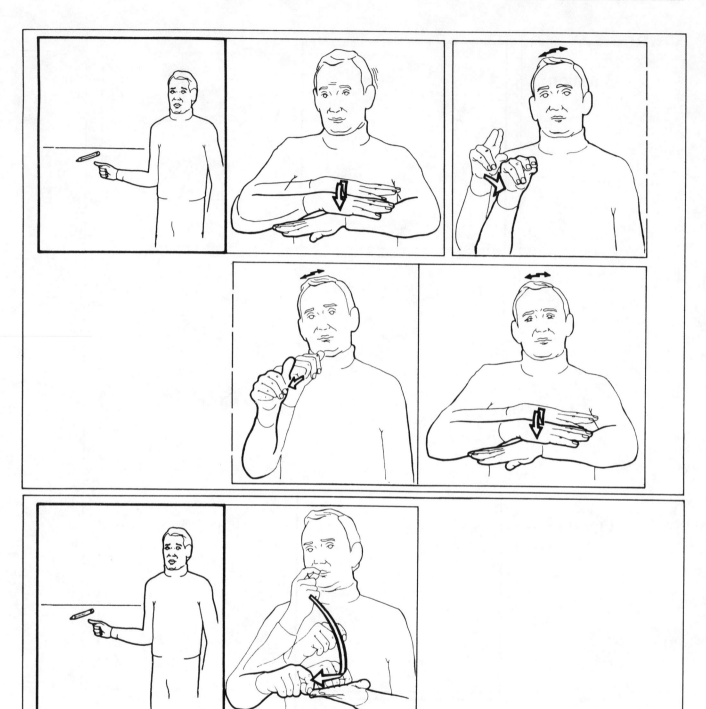

Vocabulary

Vocabulary (continued)

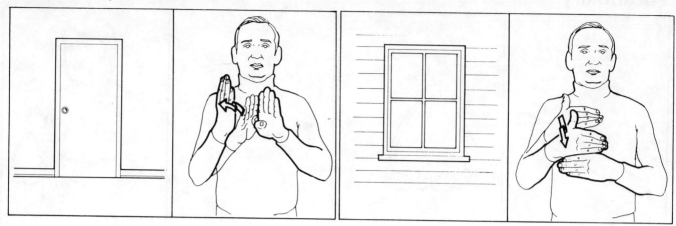

Pluralization of Nouns

There are two basic ways that nouns can be made plural in ASL.

There is a small group of nouns which can be made plural by repeating them. Two examples are:

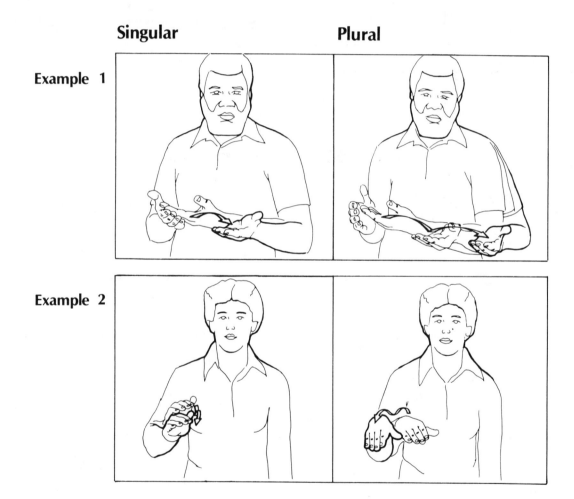

Singular   Plural

Example 1

Example 2

However a much more common way is by using a number sign, either a definite number (two, five, fifty-six) or an indefinite number (few, many, several) before or after the noun.

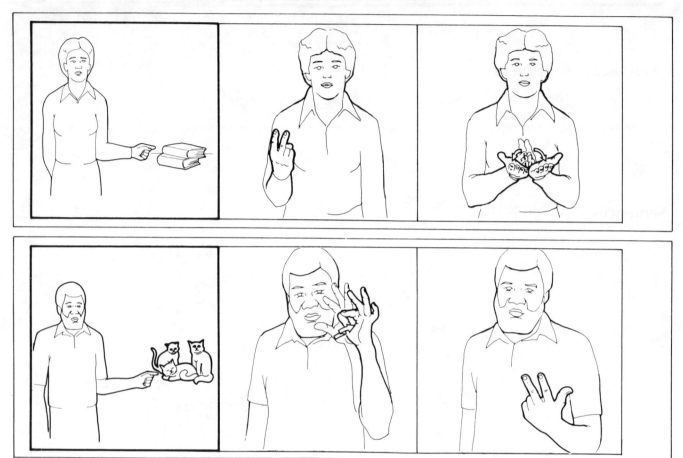

Practice yes/no questions, wh questions and pluralizing nouns by asking a friend about the following pictures, using the sentences on the next two pages as models:

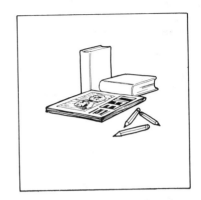

Sentences

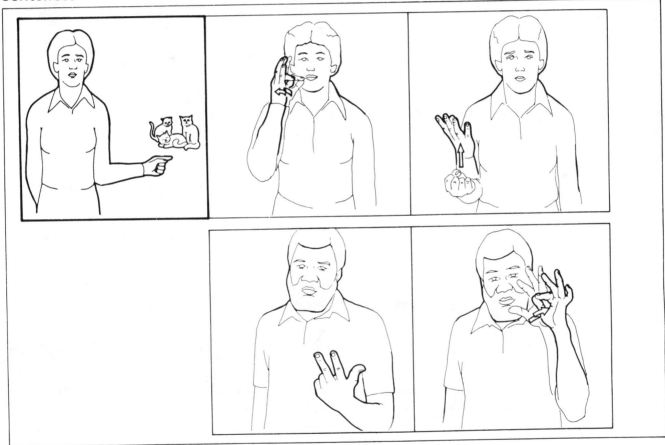

Sentences (continued)

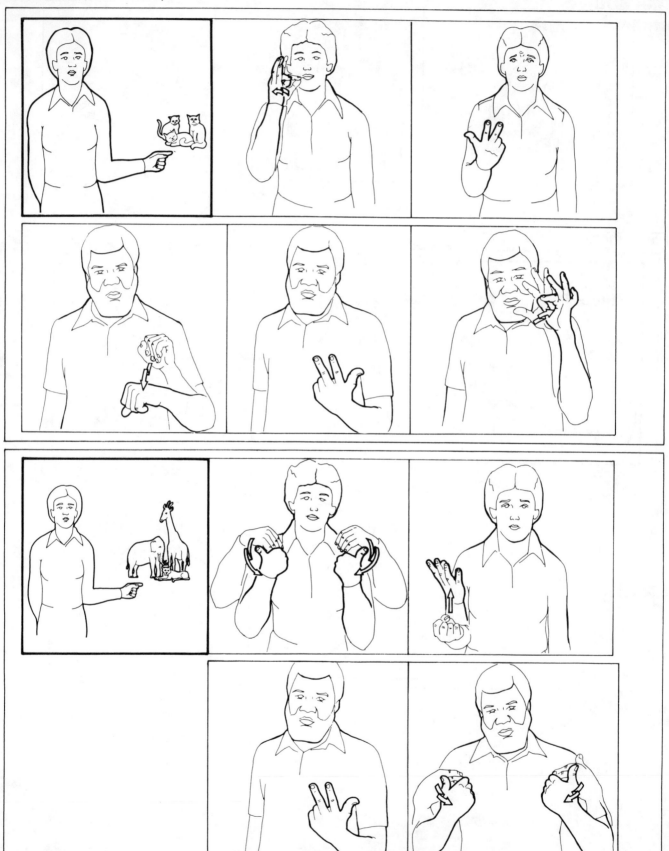

Vocabulary

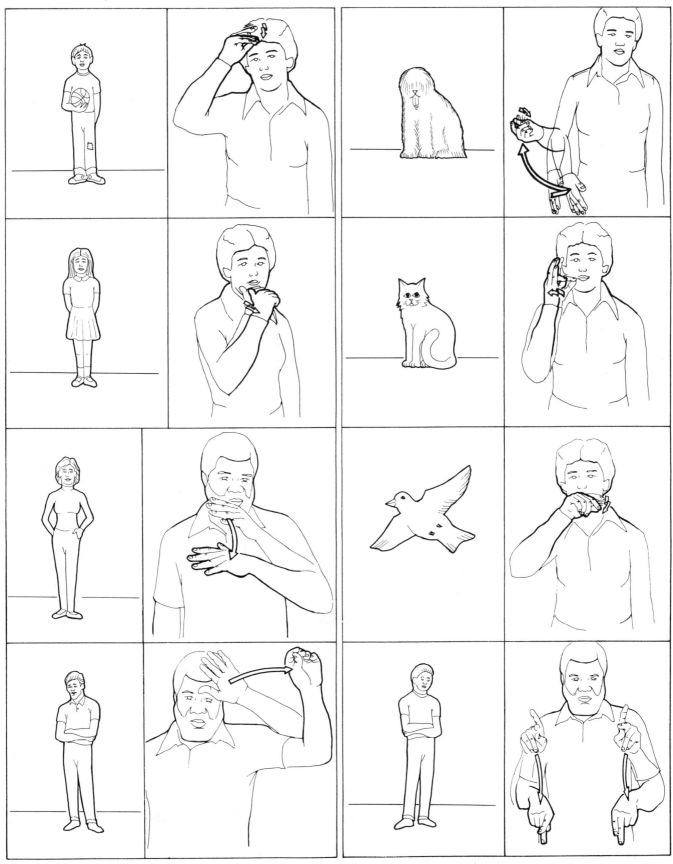

Vocabulary (continued)

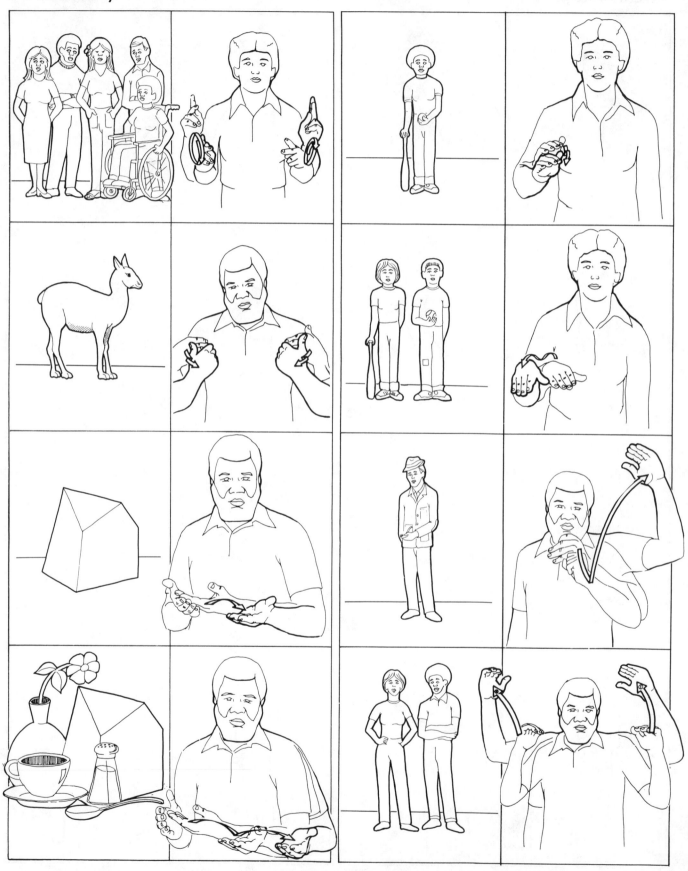

Vocabulary (continued)

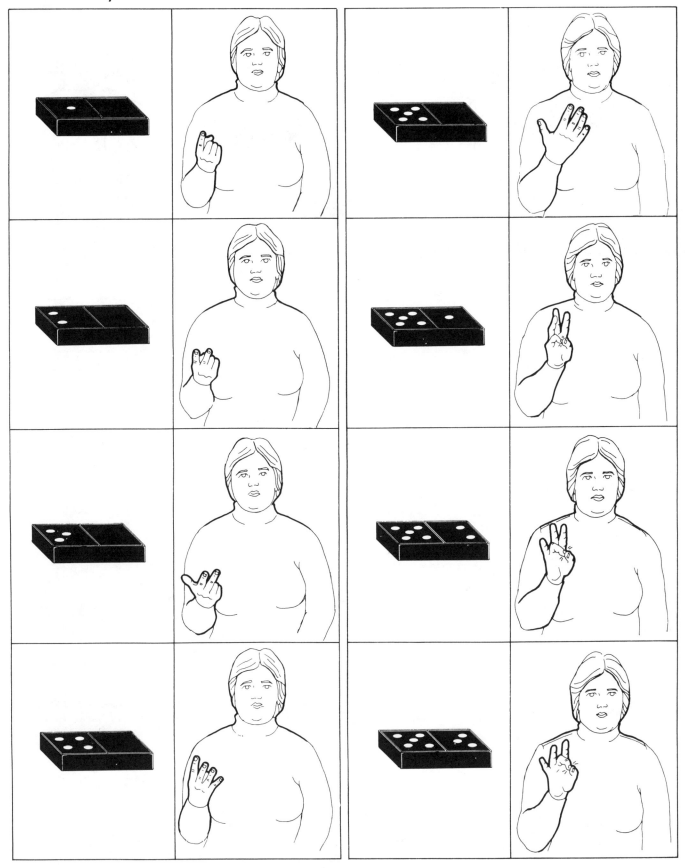

Vocabulary (continued)

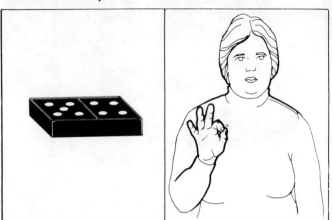

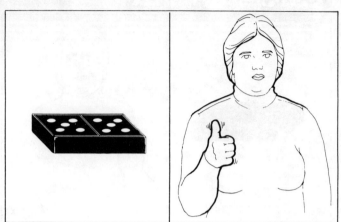

Pronominalization

In ASL, pronouns can be made either manually using a sign, or non-manually, and, as with any language, can refer to people, places or things present or not present to the speaker.

Indicating referents that are actually present is called "real world indexing." For example, suppose a signer is talking with someone about a third person who is in the room. The third person is referred to this way:

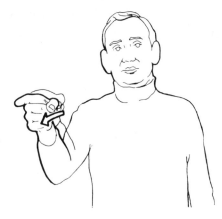

If the signer wishes to refer to two other people, the handshape is changed to:

To indicate three people, the sign changes to:

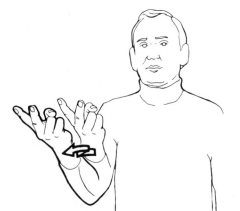

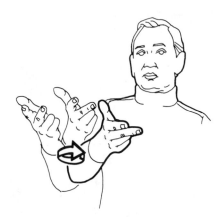

(Notice that the pronoun has now become plural).

Numbers of people up to five can be indexed this way.

To indicate several people this sign is used:

If the signer wishes to index herself she signs:

herself and one other person:

herself and two other people:

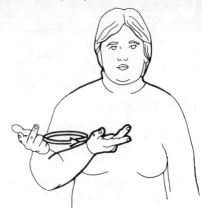

Again, numbers of people up to five can be indicated this way.

For several people who are present, including the signer, the sign . . .

is used. If the signer is talking about himself and people who are not present, the sign is slightly different:

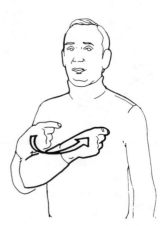

Pronouns for people or things not present are made by indicating places in the signing space which then come to stand for the persons, places or things to which the signer is referring. The handshape remains the same, but the movement can be slightly altered (as in the last example). Because the signer doesn't have to indicate referents that are actually present, the placing of referents may be closer to the signer's body. For example:

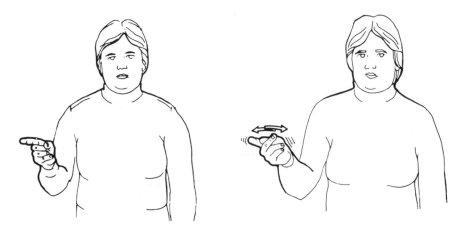

Eye gaze is an important part of pronominal reference in ASL. It can be used alone to indicate 2nd person singular when asking a question of another person, as was seen in Lesson 2. It can be used together with a manual signal to index 3rd persons, and can also be used alone for this purpose. When used without a manual signal, a slight tilt of the head toward the person(s) being indexed usually accompanies the eye-indexing. If one wishes to index a 3rd person, and doesn't want that person to know they are being discussed, eye indexing is often used alone, and the head tilt if present at all is very slight.

Pronoun Copy

In ASL subject and object pronouns can be optionally copied (signed again) at the end of a sentence. Here are some examples.

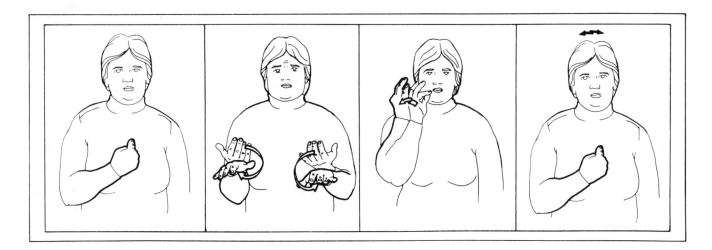

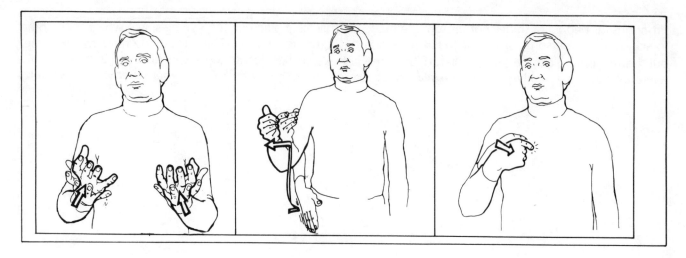

Signs for wh questions can also appear at 1) the beginning of a sentence 2) the end of a sentence 3) both the beginning and the end of a sentence. Some examples are:

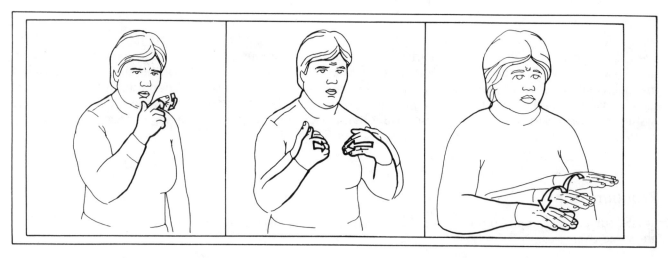

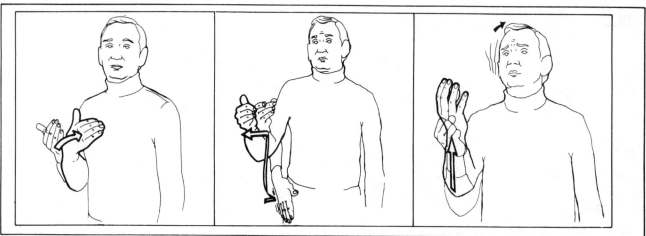

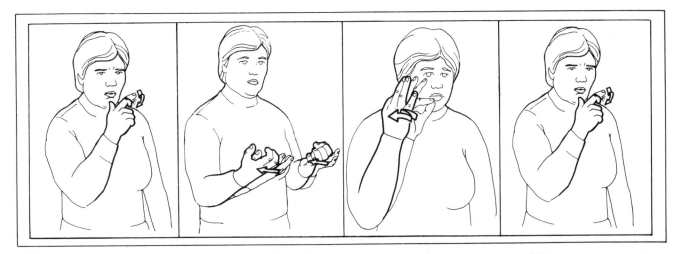

Practice using these sentence patterns by modeling the sentences in the examples and using vocabulary from the lessons.

Directional Verbs: The Incorporation of Subject and Object Pronouns

In ASL the movement of some verbs can be changed to show the direction of an action, that is, to show who is doing what to whom. These verbs are called directional verbs, and when using them one doesn't need separate signs for pronouns because one knows who is doing the action (the subject) and who is receiving the action (the object or indirect object) by the way the verb is moved. The pronouns are thus incorporated into the verb. Some examples are:

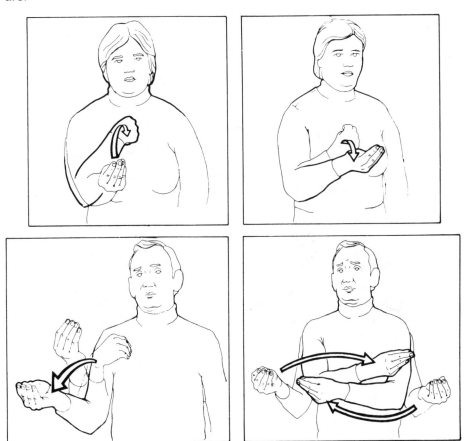

Incorporation of Negation Into Verbs

There is a very small group of verbs which can, by a change in the direction in which they are made, include negation in the verb sign itself. A manual signal indicating negation is not needed when using these verbs in their negated form, but non-manual signals indicating negation almost always occur. An example from this lesson is:

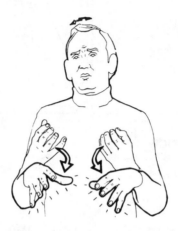

Practice using the grammar and vocabulary you have learned with the following pictures:

Vocabulary

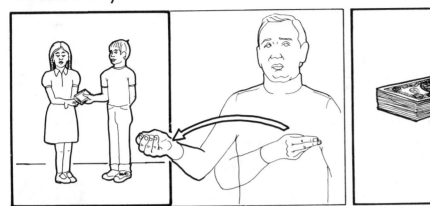

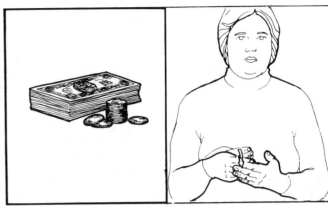

Definitions

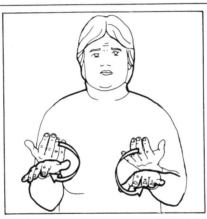

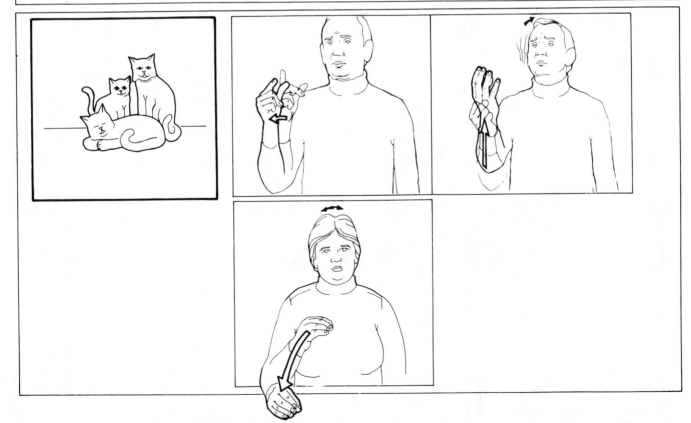

Definitions (continued)

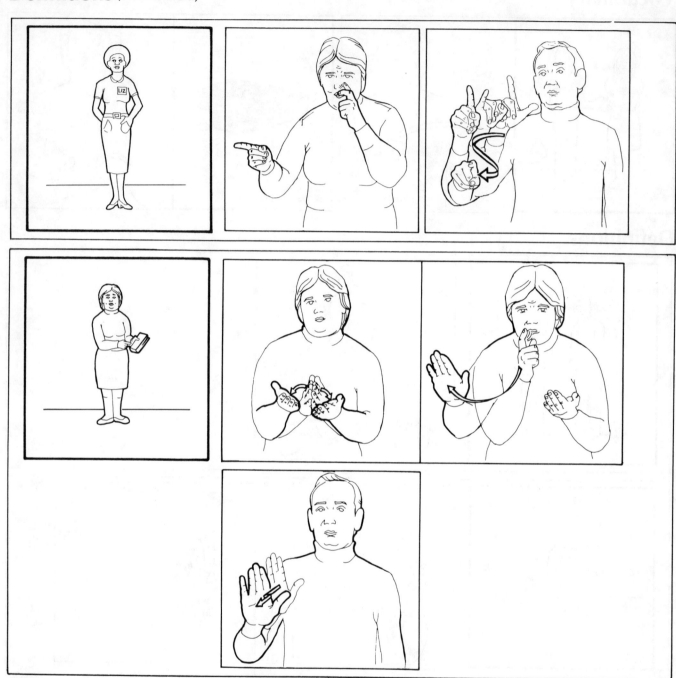

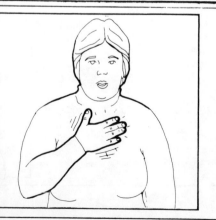

Definitions (continued)

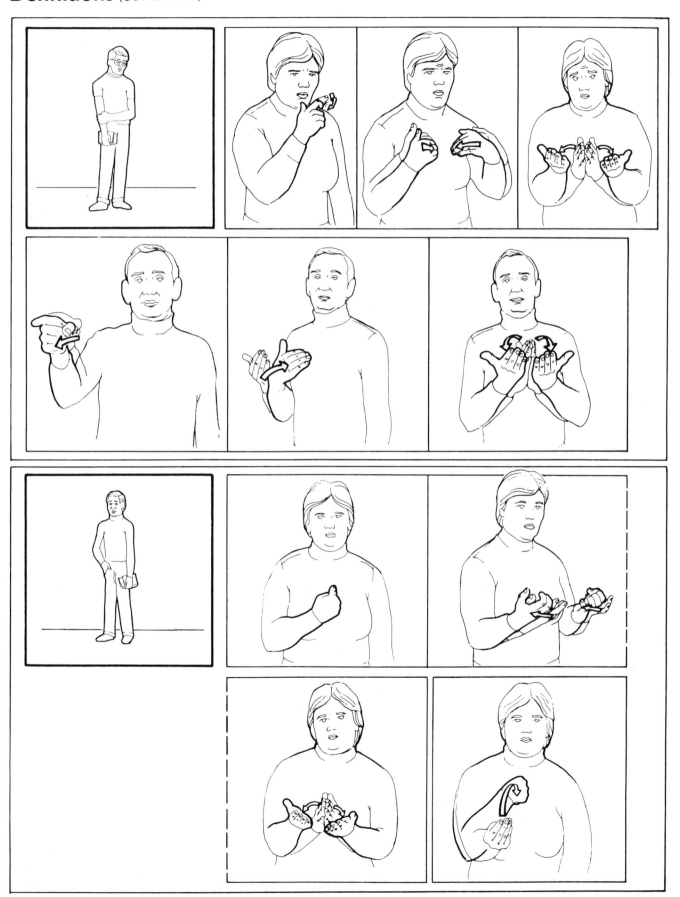

Inflection of Verbs: Manner

In the sentence "The woman walked quickly down the lane." the word "quickly" is an adverb. It tells us how the woman walked.

ASL often inflects the verb; that is, signers can change the manner in which the verb is signed to indicate how something is done. Here are some examples. The first is uninflected, the second two are inflected.

No Inflection

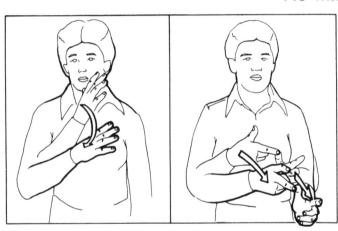
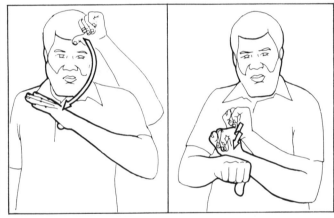

Inflection: fast

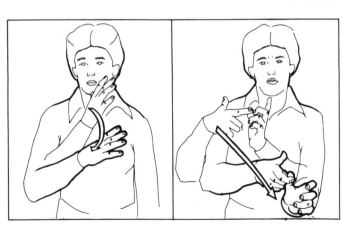
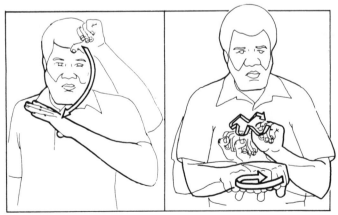

Inflection: fast (non-manual signal: intense)

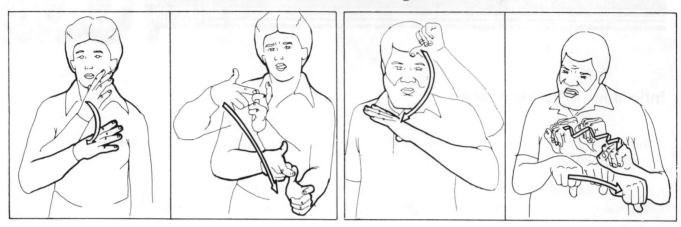

Notice the non-manual grammatical signal used in the third part of each example. This signal is used to show that the action is more intense than it usually is.

Answer the following question:

about each of the following pictures:

Vocabulary

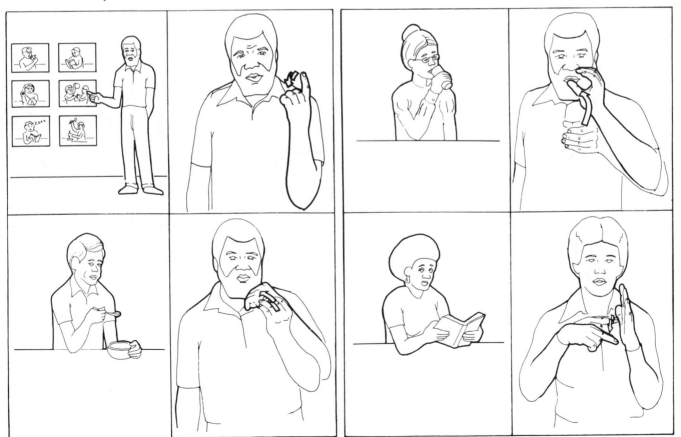

Vocabulary (continued)

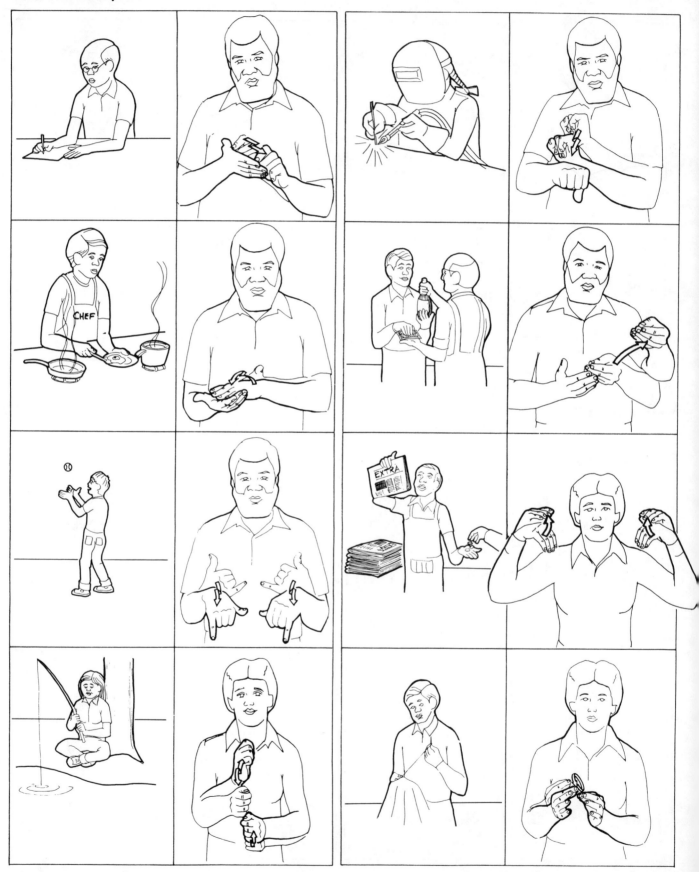

Vocabulary (continued)

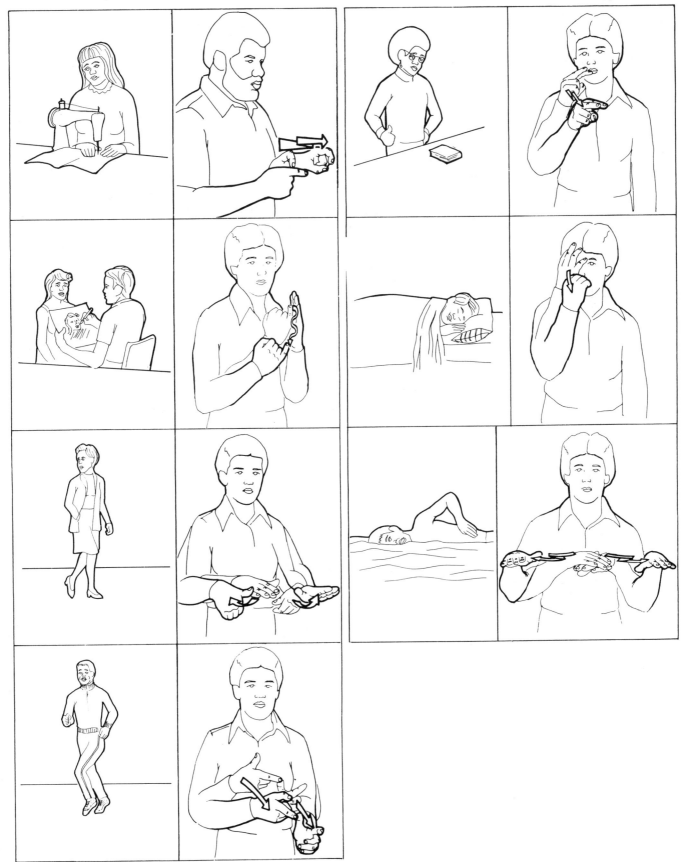

Definitions: (continued)

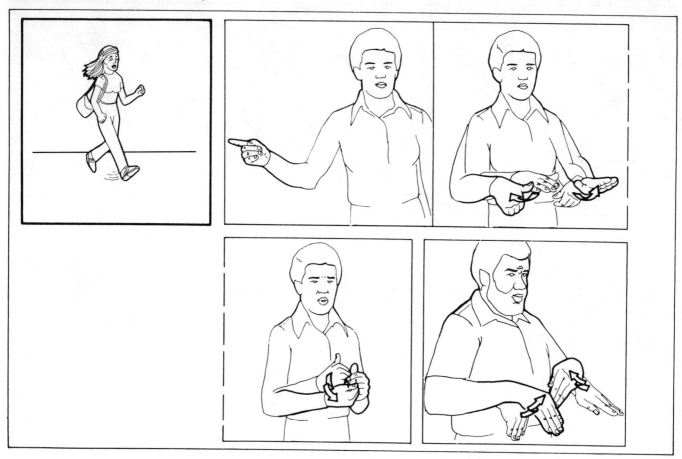

GRAMMAR

The Time Line

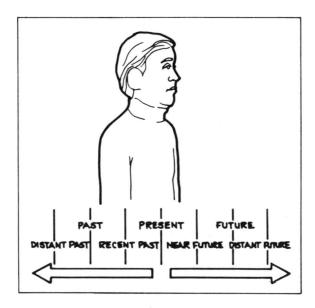

The "time line" is an imaginary line running through the signer's body and extending to the front and back of the signer. Signs which refer to the future move forward along the time line; signs which refer to the past move backward along it. Signs referring to the present are made close to the body. Signs indicating only a few days into the past or furure are also made close to the body, but they move in either a backward or forward direction, depending on whether they refer to the past or the future.

Closeness and Distance in Time

A signer, when talking about an event, can modify a time sign to show how close in time to the present the event happened or will happen. For example, if I am promising you that I will read the book just as soon as I have finished lunch, the sign I use to indicate time will be made closer to my body than if, for example, I intend to read the book next week or next month. In addition, there is a non-manual grammatical signal that indicates closeness in time:

Example 1

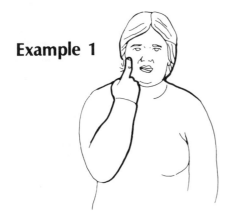

Example 2

Both drawings show a sign referring the the past with the non-manual adverbial signal indicating closeness in time, but **#2** is more intense. The more intense the signal, the closer in time to the present is the event that has occurred or will occur.

There are also non-manual signals to indicate distant past or future:

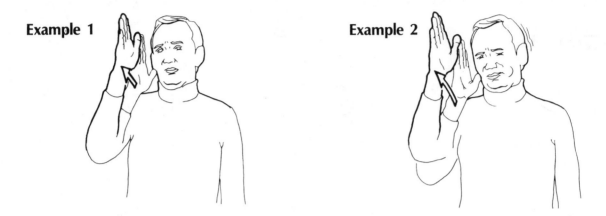

Example 1   **Example 2**

The different non-manual signals indicate a different distance into the past or future. Which signal looks more intense? It is the one in Example 2. With the signal for closeness in time, the more intense signal indicated an event's closer proximity to the present; with events happening in the distant past or future, the more intense the signal, the farther away in time it occurred or will occur.

Tense of Verbs

In ASL the form of the verb does not change to indicate tense. Instead we know what tense the verb has because other signs give us that information. In ASL, once the time frame has been established, the people having the conversation know when the events being discussed will happen or have happened, and the verb does not need to change to provide that information.

Signs that give us this information about when something happened and help establish the tense of verbs are sometimes called "time indicator" signs, and often appear near the beginning of a sentence.

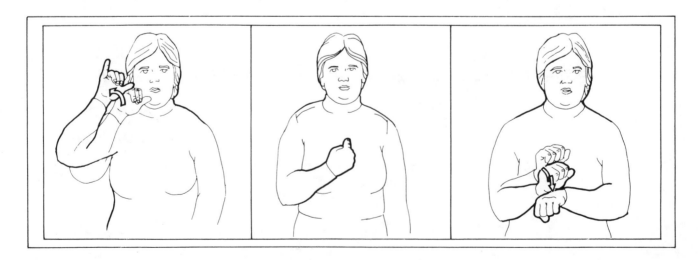

They can also appear at the end of the sentence, especially if the sentence is a short, declarative one.

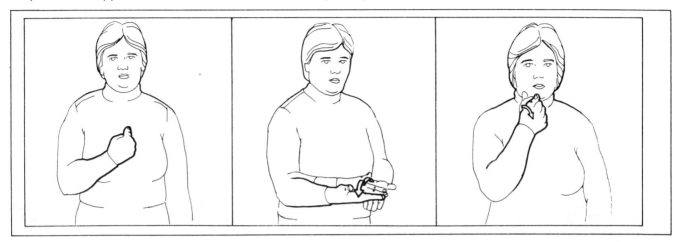

After the time is indicated, everything from then on is presumed to be happening in the same time frame. If the signer wants to change the time frame, another time sign will be used:

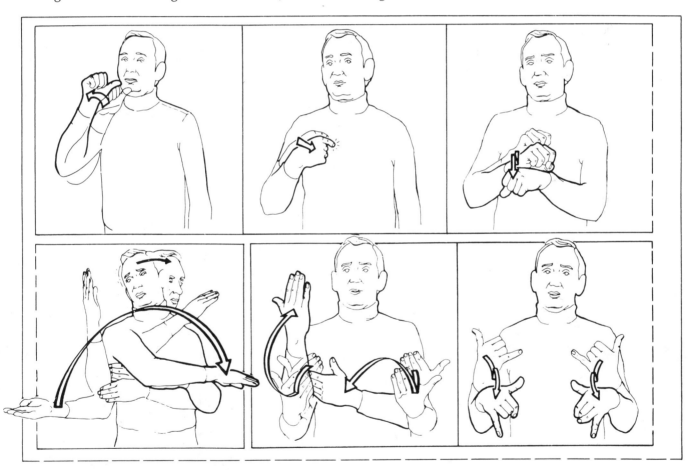

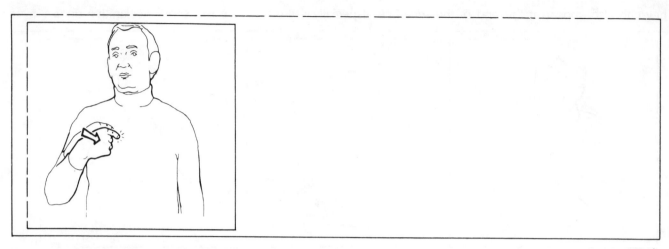

Time can also be understood from context. In the example just given, suppose two people were talking at noon. Then they would know that the time frame of the 2nd sentence was past tense. If they happened to be talking at 8 AM, the activity referred to (probably) hasn't happened yet.

If the signer in this example wanted to be especially clear or emphatic he might sign:

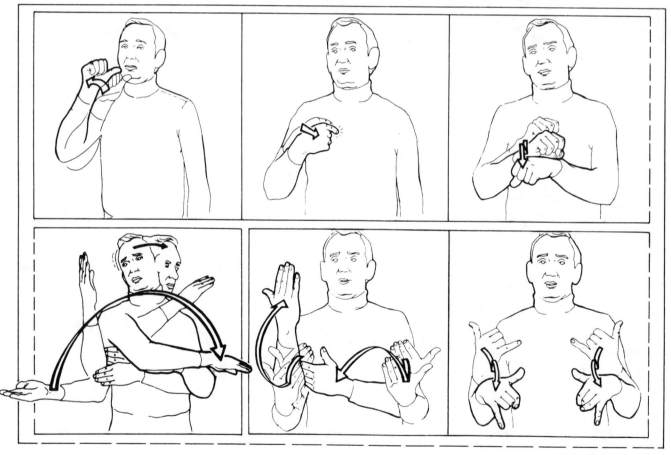

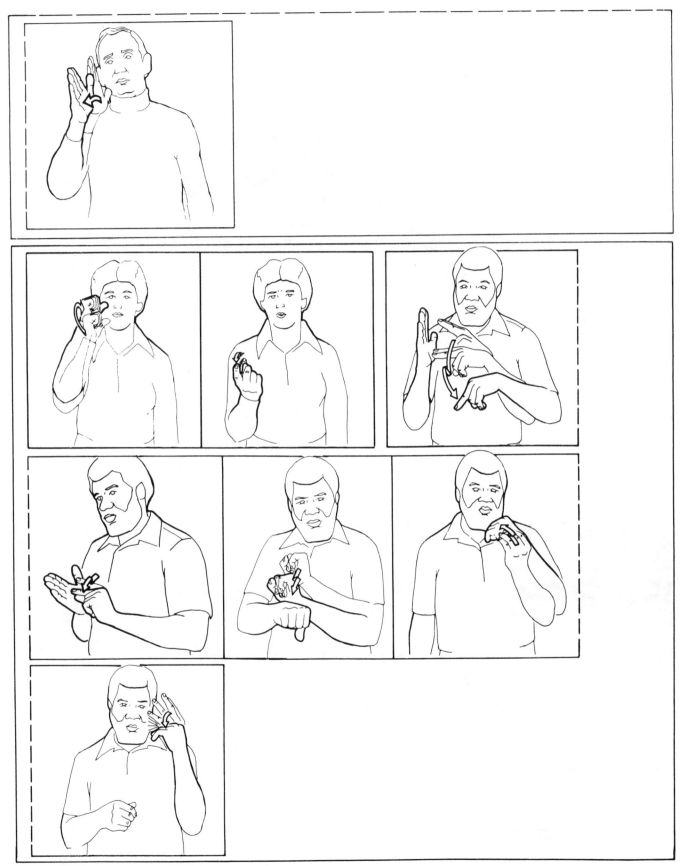

With longer or more complex sentences, time indicator signs are more likely to occur at the beginning of the sentence, or in the first clause of the sentence.

Practice establishing time frames using the time indicator signs in this lesson. Use the sentences in the preceding pages as models.

Vocabulary

Vocabulary (continued)

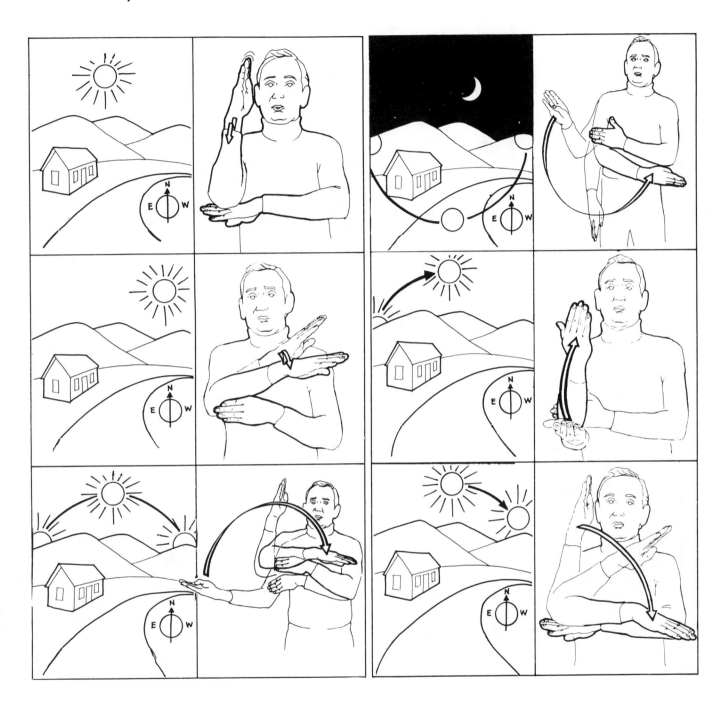

Definitions

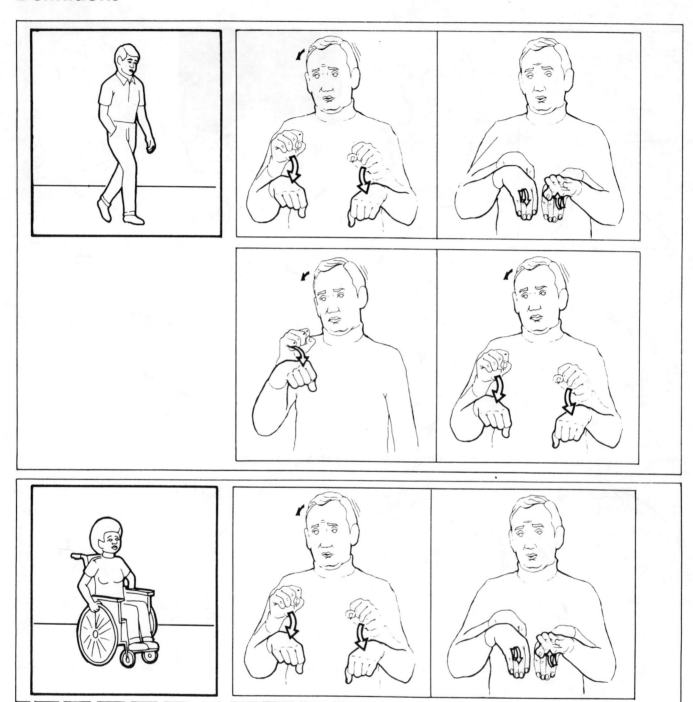

Definitions (continued)

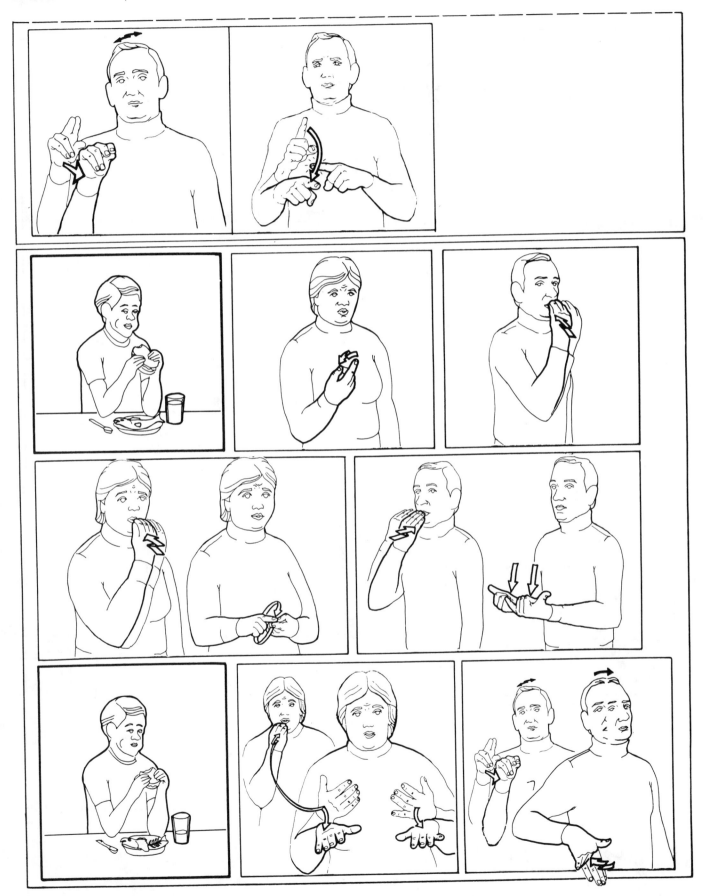

Definitions: (continued)

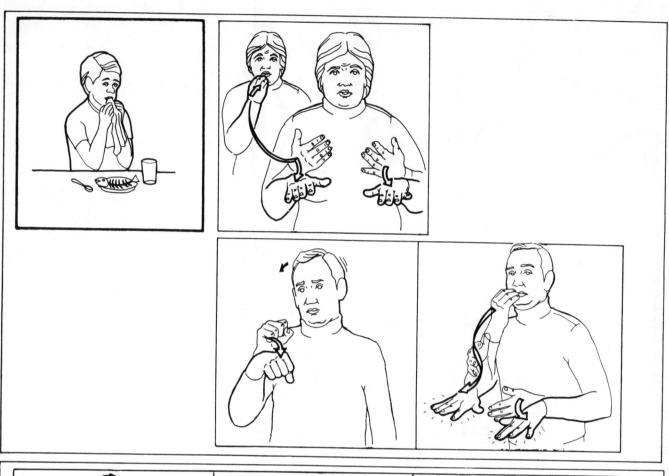

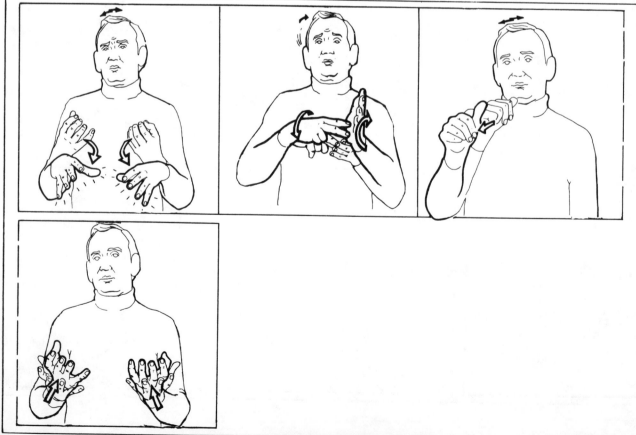

Definitions (continued)

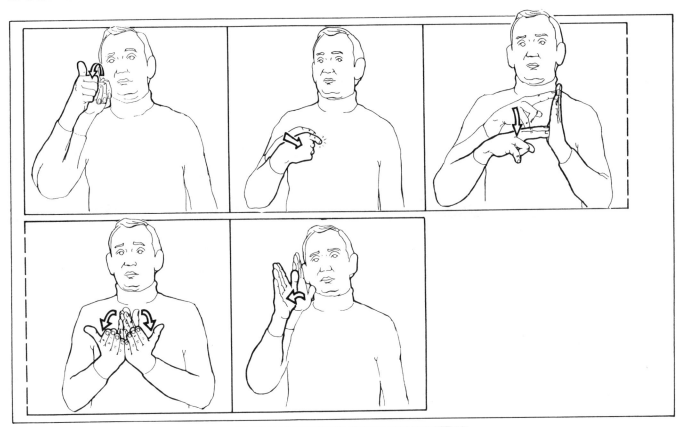

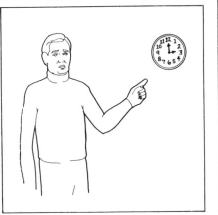

Conjunctions: Indexing on the Non-Dominant Hand

When ASL signers have more than two items to conjoin they may choose to index them on the non-dominant hand. (The dominant hand is the one a signer uses to make one-handed signs, and the hand that moves in those two-handed signs where one hand (the non-dominant hand) acts as a base).

An example of this kind of indexing is:

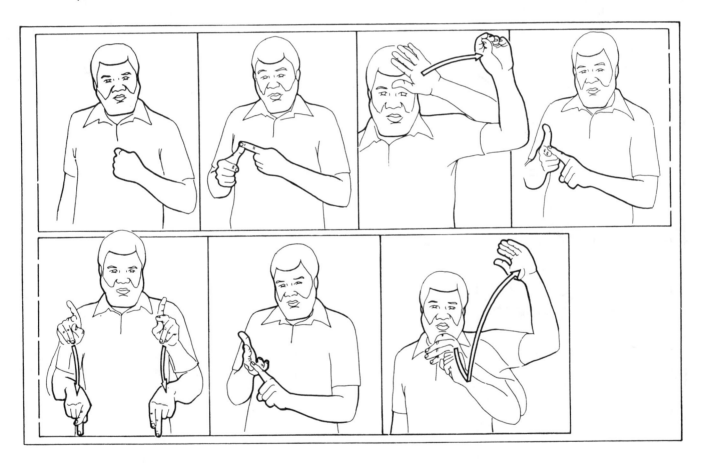

Practice indexing on your non-dominant hand using the following sentences as models.

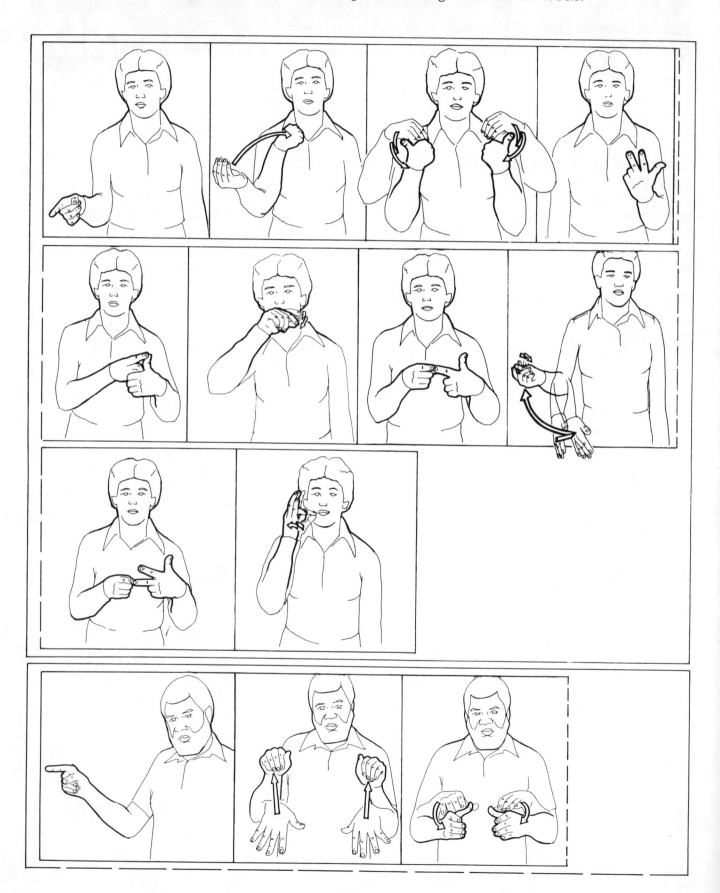

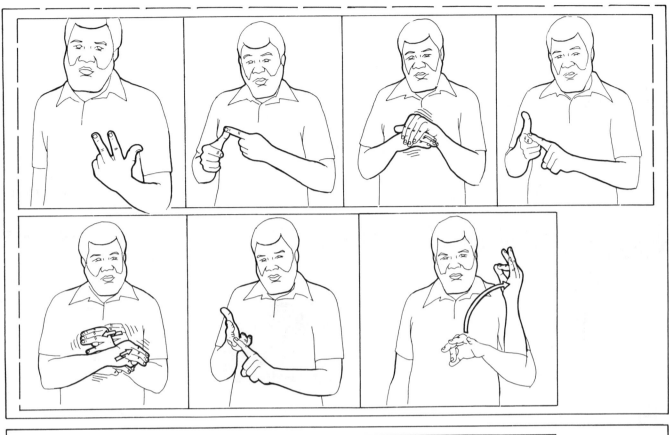

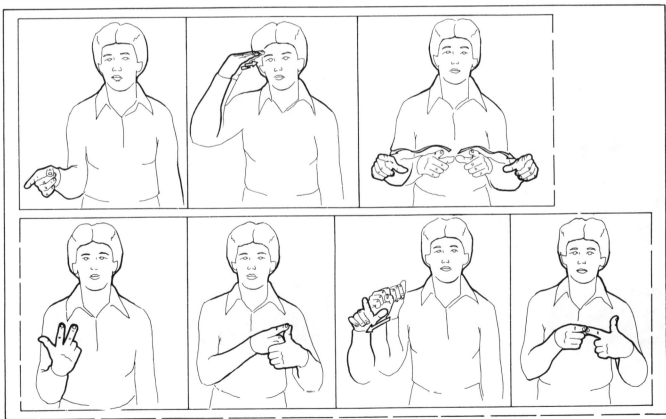

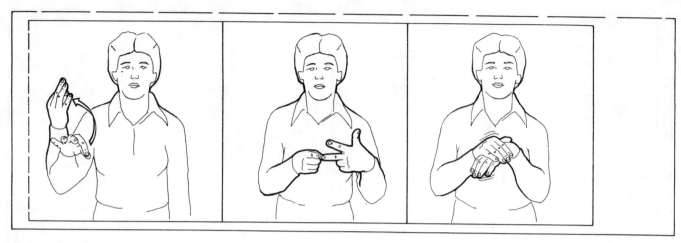

Vocabulary

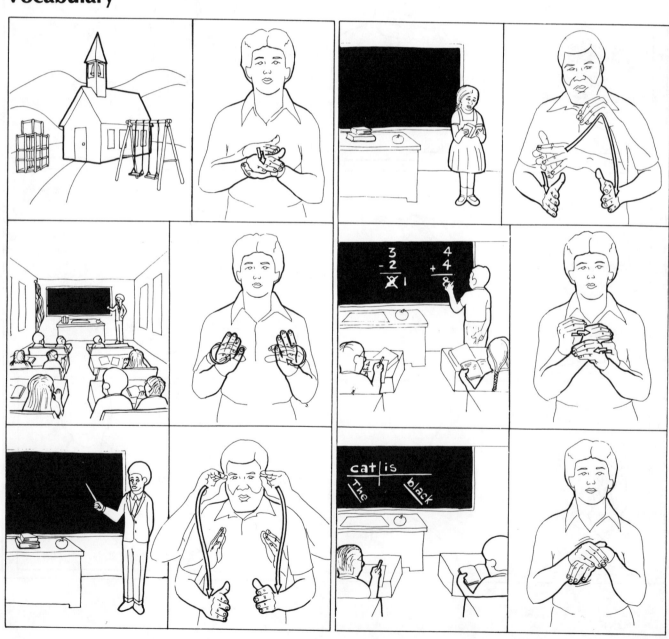

Vocabulary (continued)

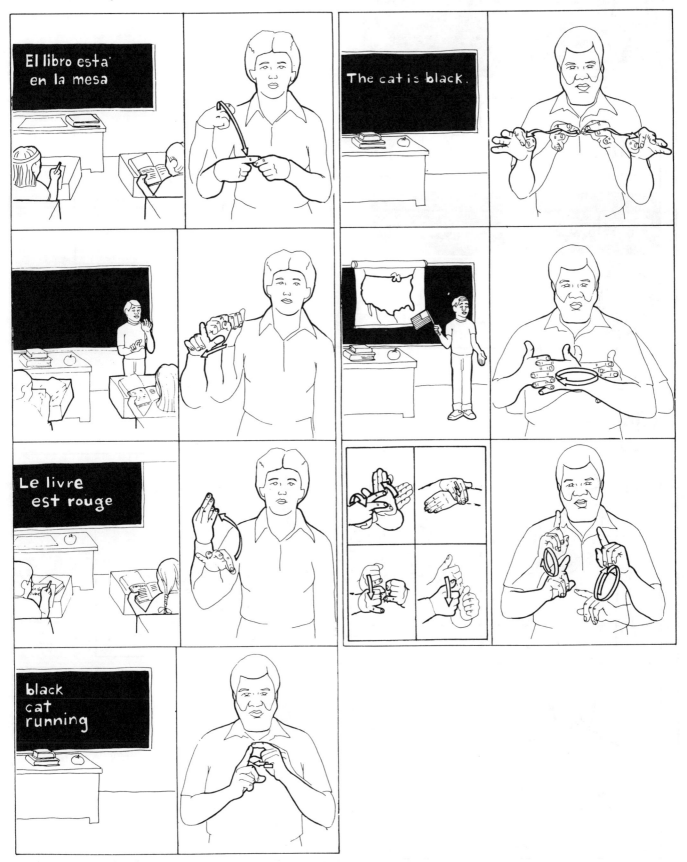

Definitions

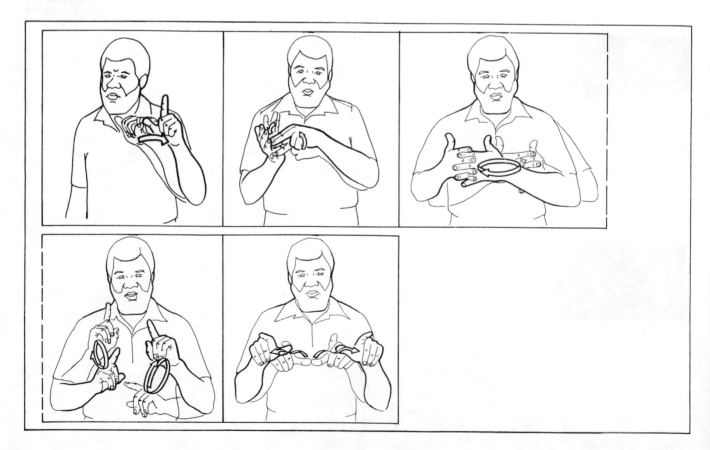

Definitions (continued)

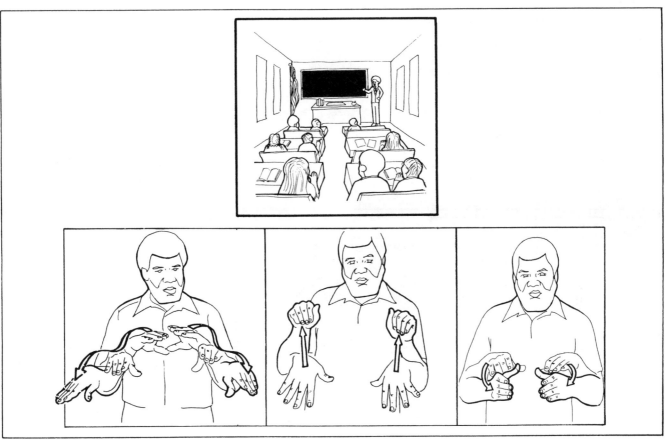

Definitions (continued)

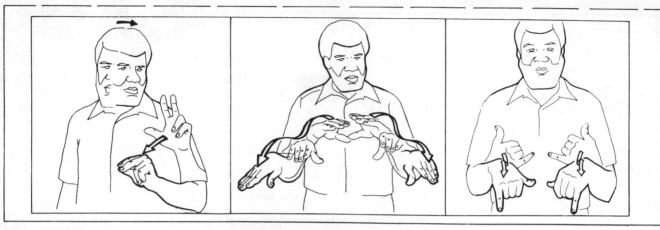

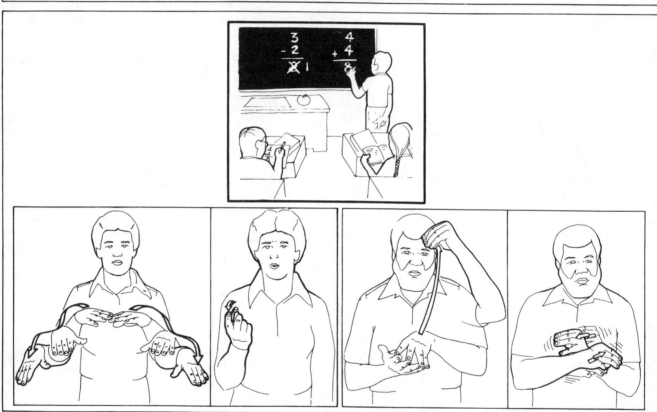

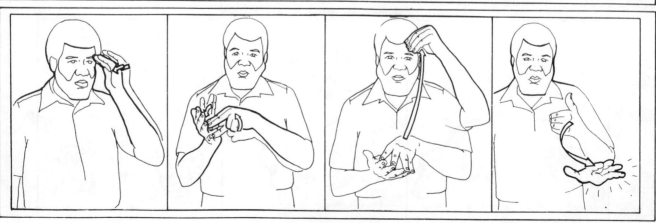

Pluralization: Indefinite Quantifiers

Lesson 2 showed pluralization with definite numbers. Pluralization with indefinite quantifiers is similar and can occur before or after the noun. Some examples are:

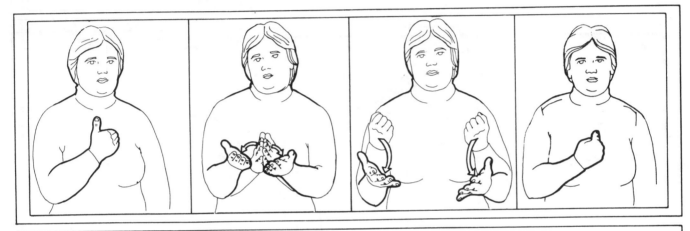

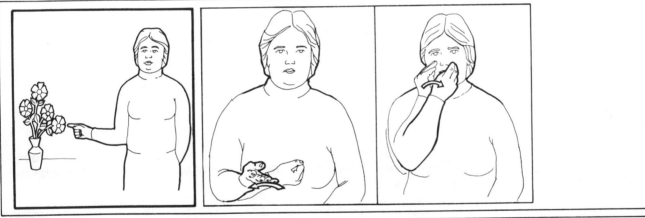

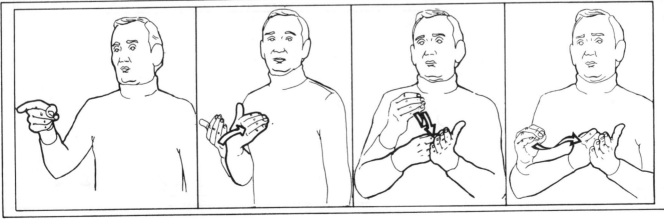

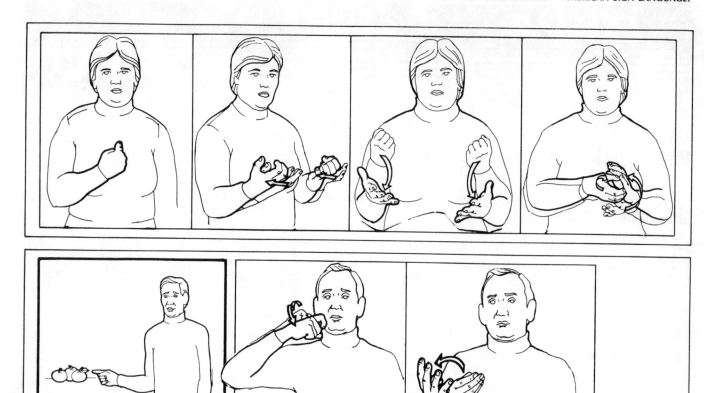

Practice forming sentences with indefinite quantifiers, using the vocabulary from the lessons and the sentences above as models.

Topicalization

Topicalization occurs when speakers first mention the topic they wish to discuss, and then make some comment on it. ASL signers often use this sentence structure, which has a different word order from the subject-verb-object word order we have already seen as in:

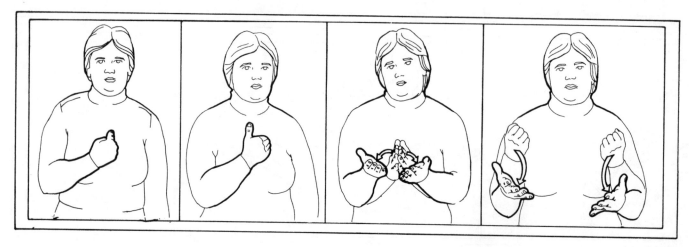

In topicalized sentences the order is:

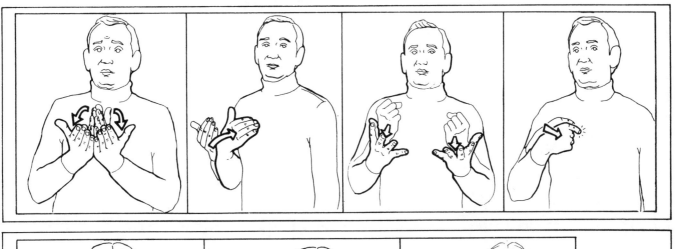

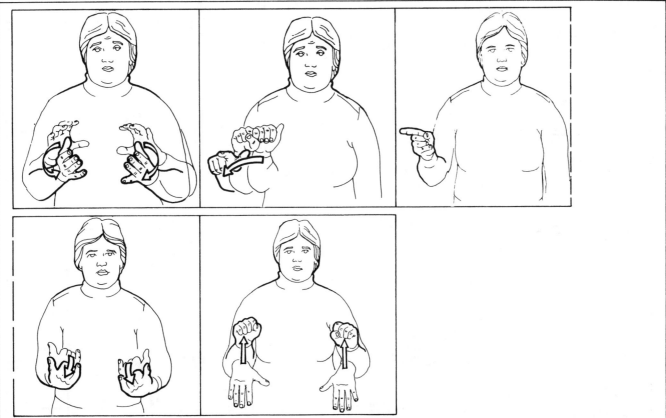

In this order the object is signed first and a non-manual grammatical signal, called a topic marker or topic signal, accompanies it. (Notice the difference in the facial expressions of the signer in the last sentence shown on the previous page, and for those above.)

Practice this topic-comment sentence pattern using the vocabulary you have learned so far. Here are some examples to use as models.

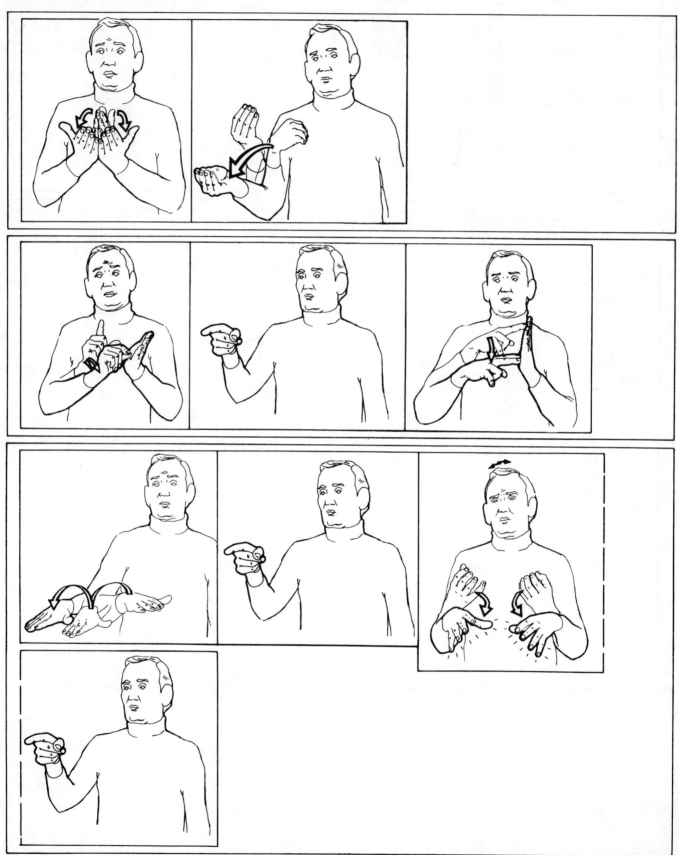

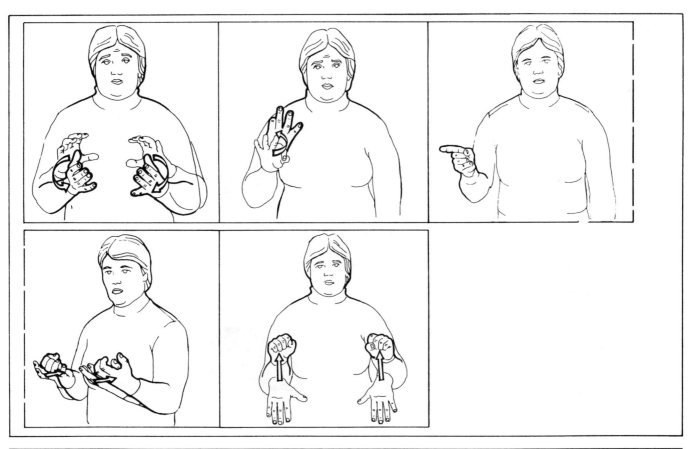

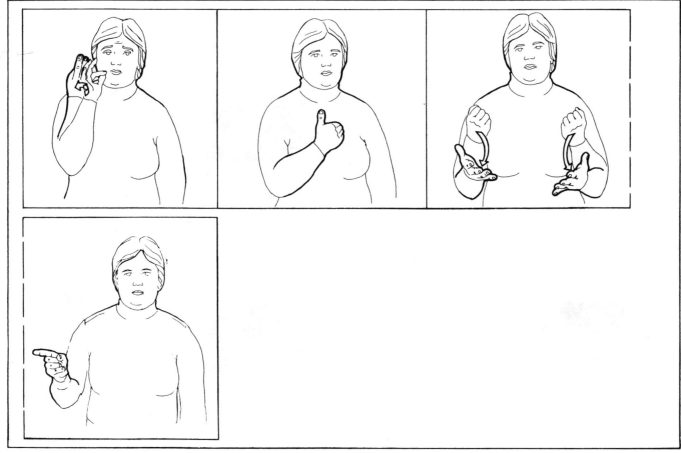

Vocabulary

Vocabulary (continued)

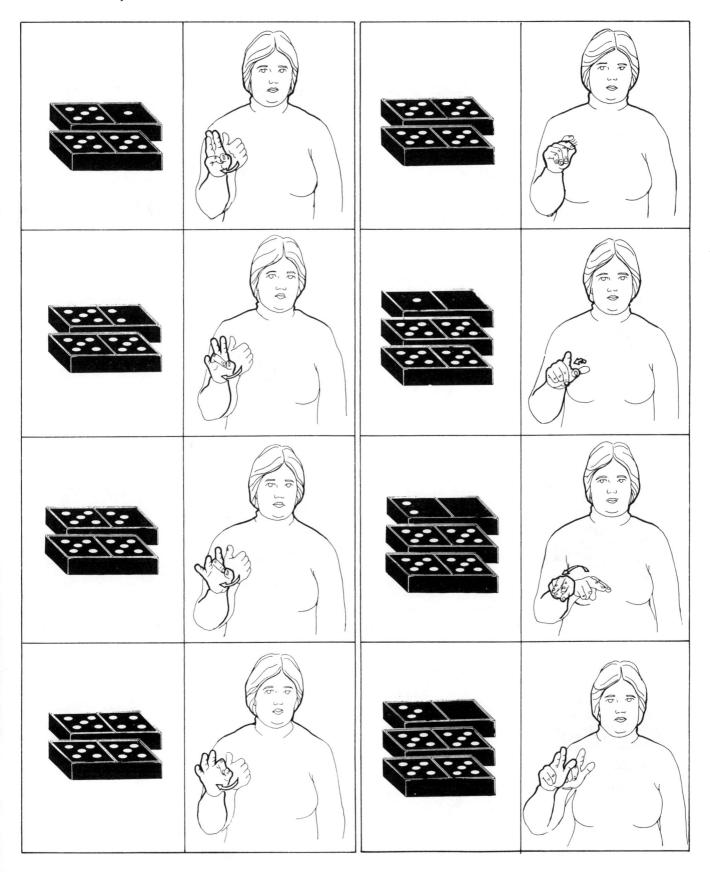

Vocabulary (continued)

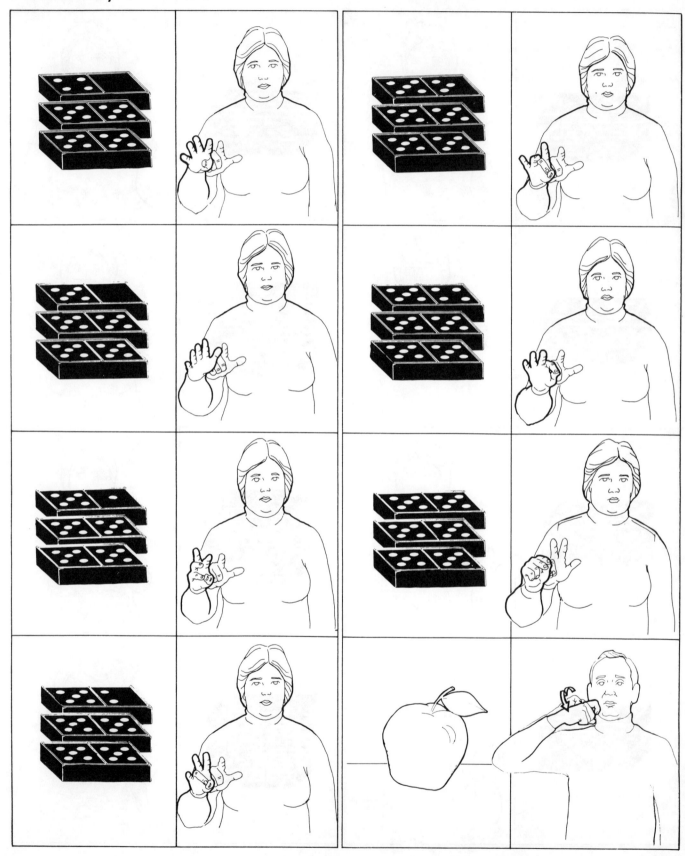

Vocabulary (continued)

Vocabulary (continued)

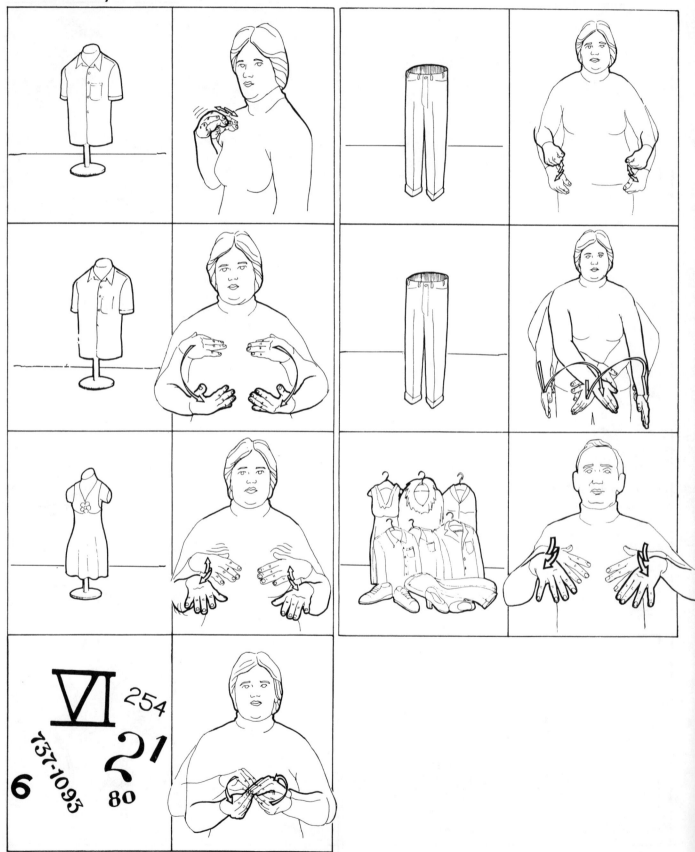

Definitions

Definitions (continued)

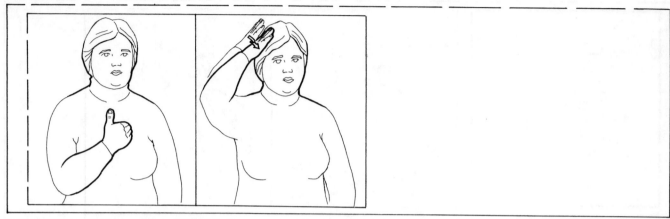

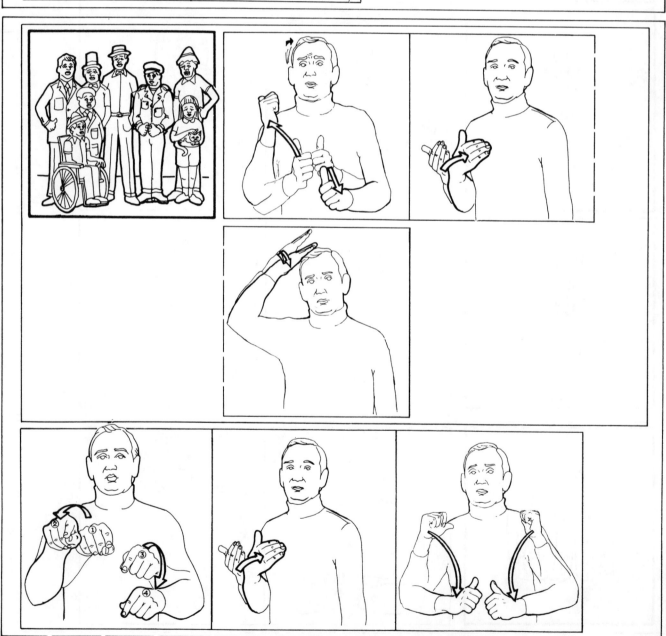

Definitions (continued)

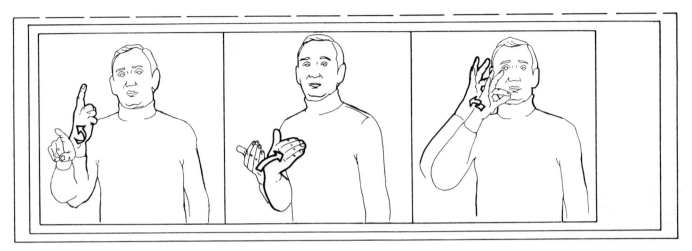

Sentence Structure

The Rhetorical Question Sentence Pattern

A rhetorical question is one to which the speaker neither expects nor wants an answer. The speaker will ask a question setting up the expectation in the addressee's mind that the information to answer the question will be forthcoming from the speaker. But how does the addressee know that it is a rhetorical question being asked, and not one to which the speaker expects an answer? Because even though wh question signs are used in the rhetorical question sentence pattern, the non-manual grammatical signal is different. The signal for wh questions can be seen in these illustrations:

For rhetorical questions the signal changes to:

Practice asking both wh questions, with the addressee answering, and rhetorical questions, with the speaker providing the answer. Here are some examples of the rhetorical question sentence pattern to use as models.

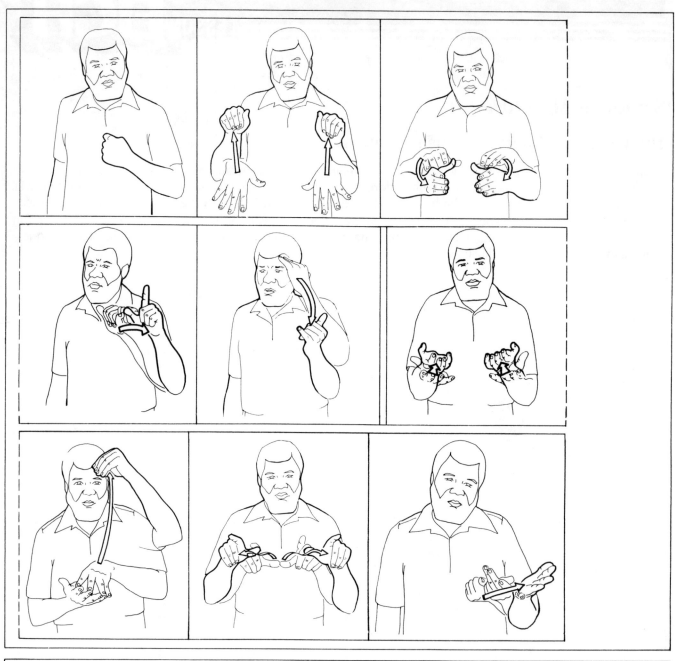

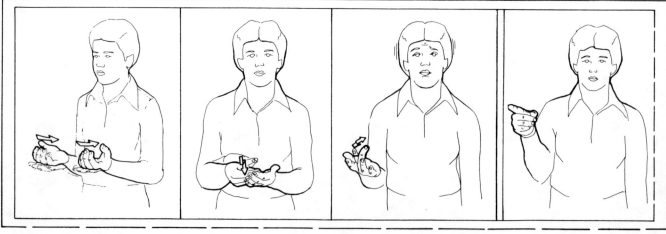

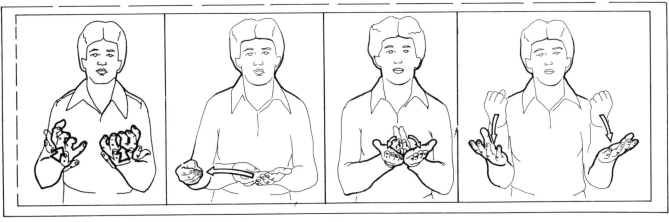

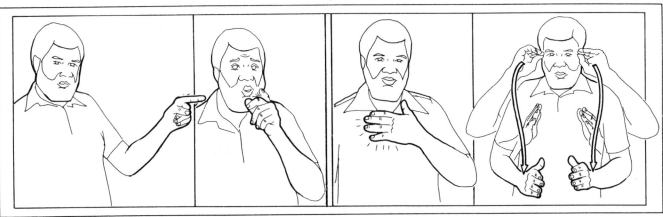

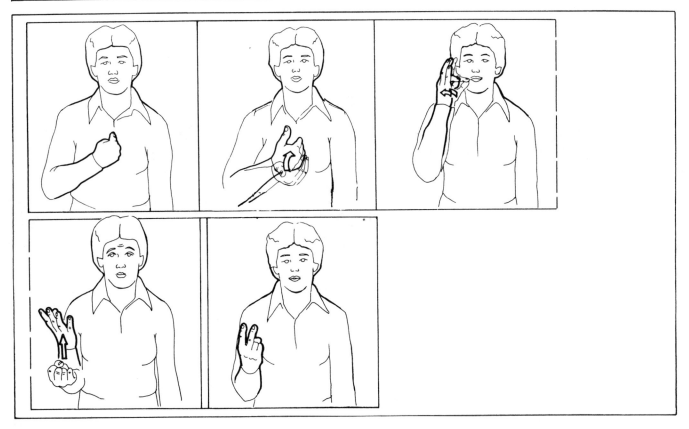

Conditional Statements

There are two parts to any conditional statement. The first expresses the condition (an "if" clause), and the second the result (a "then" clause). ASL uses a specific non-manual grammatical signal to mark conditional sentences. In conditional statements, the signal changes for the result part of the statement. Examples are:

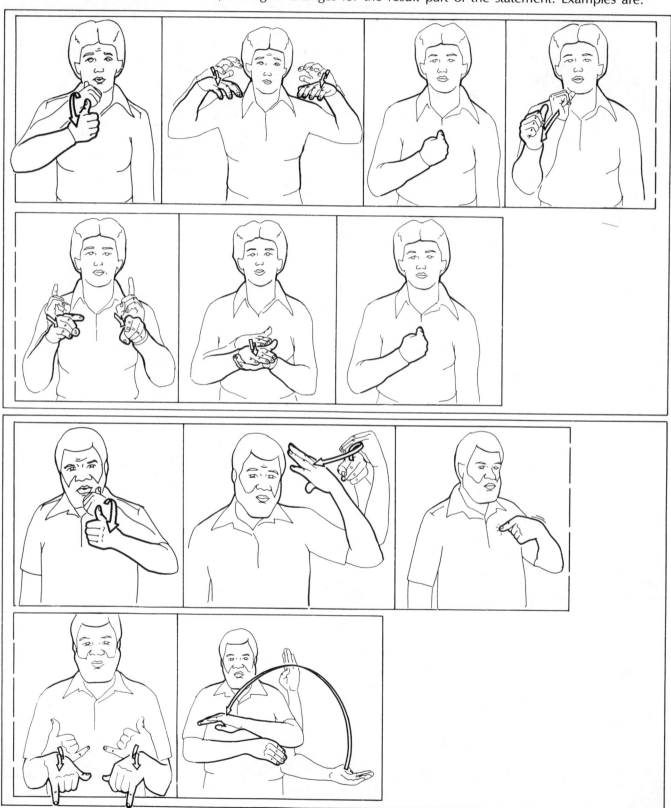

There are also two manual signs that can indicate conditional sentences.

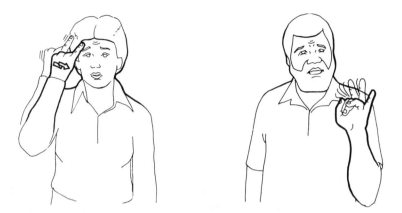

They are optionally placed at the beginning of the sentence.

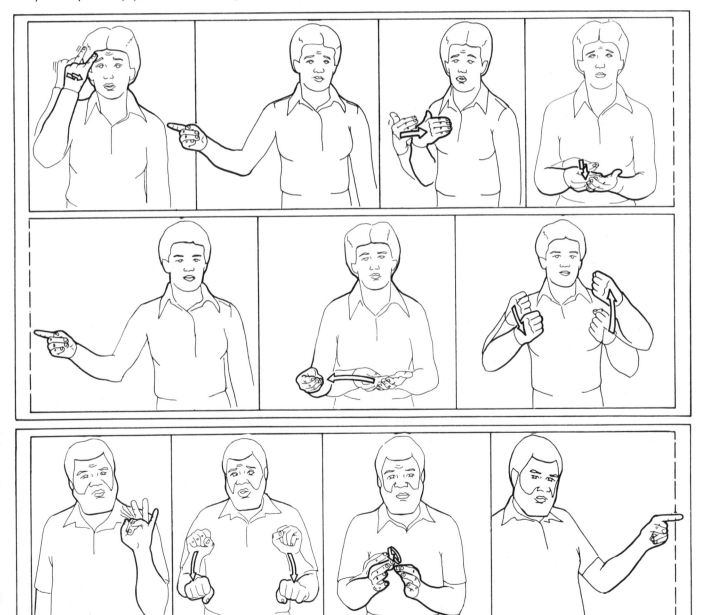

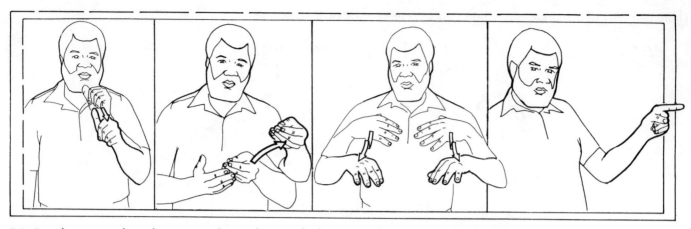

(Notice that even though a manual signal is used, the non-manual signal is still present).

Conditional Questions

With conditional sentences that are questions, the non-manual signal continues throughout the entire sentence.

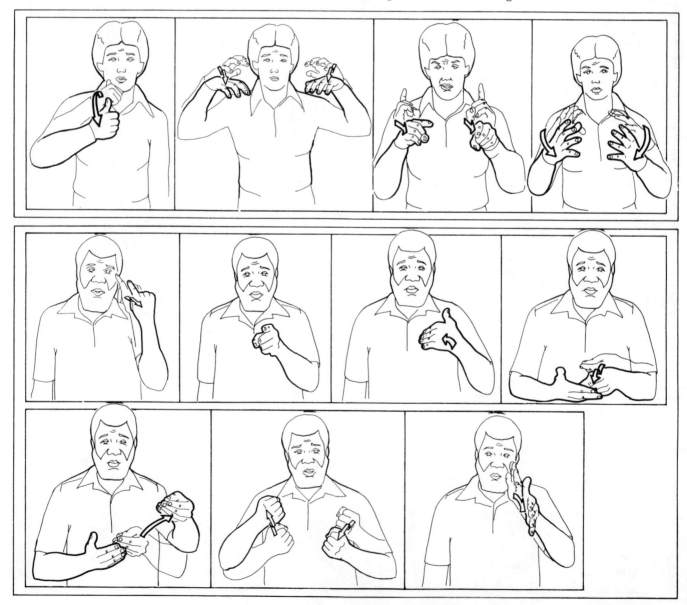

Vocabulary

Definitions

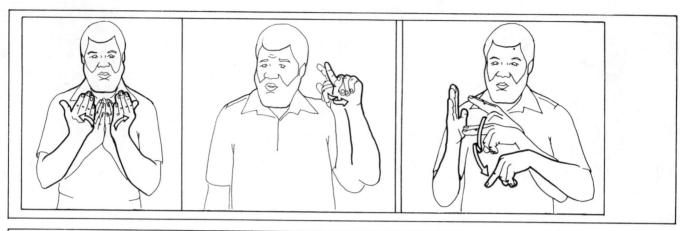

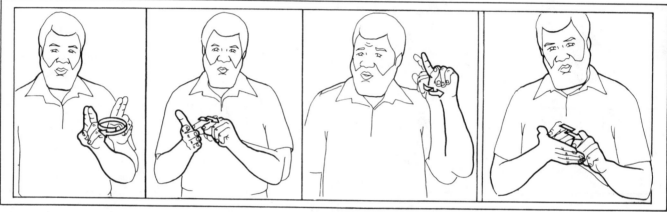

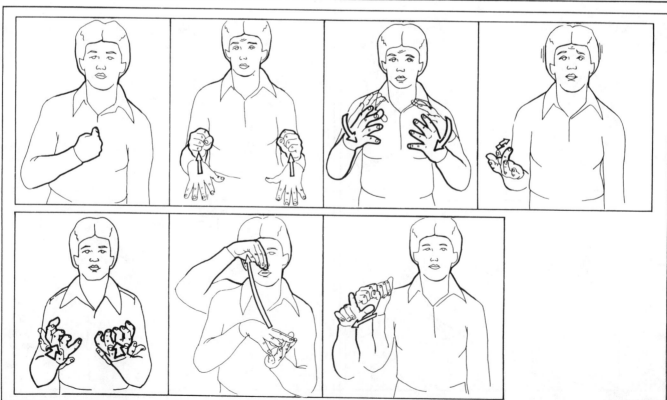

Definitions (continued)

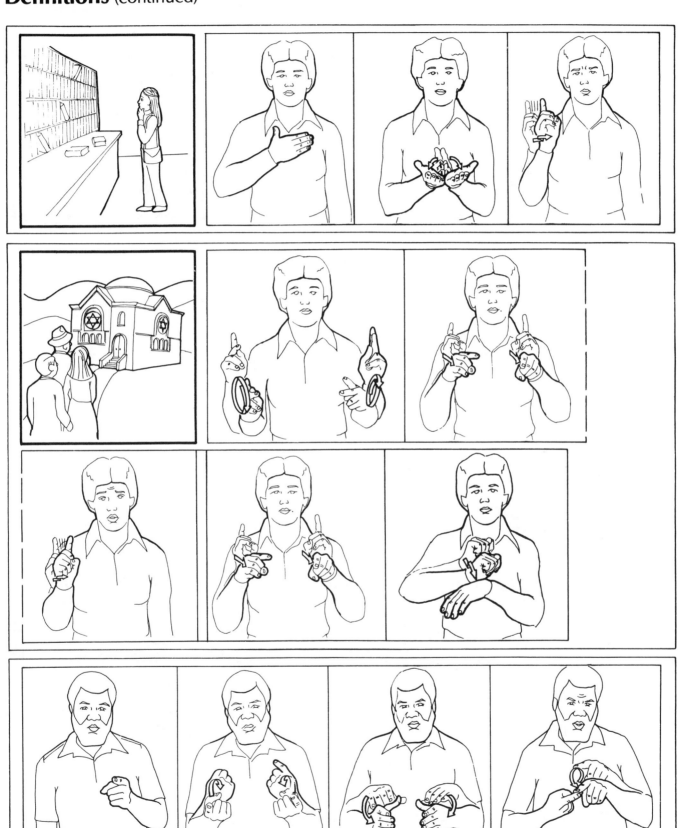

More About The Time Line

Lesson 5 introduced the imaginary time line which allows ASL signers to use space and movement to establish moments in time. This lesson includes several signs related to time, and they all follow the principles outlined in Lesson 5 explaining the time line. For example:

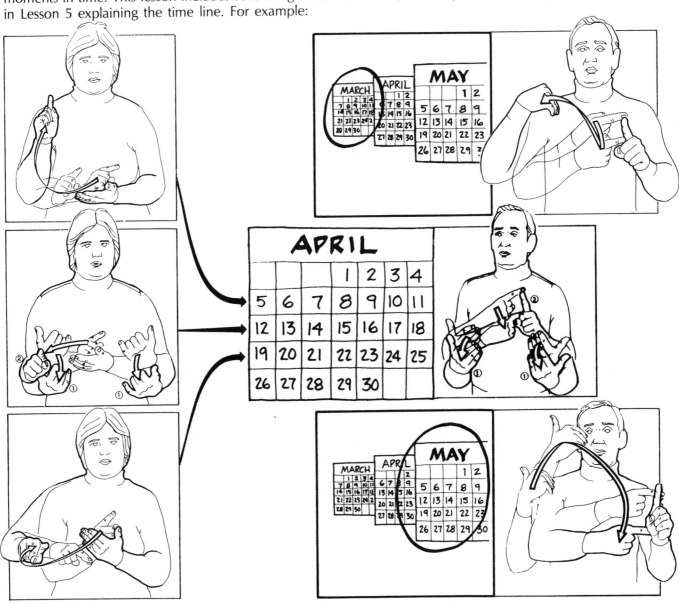

In the examples above, notice how the signs related to the future move forward away from the signer and signs related to the past move backward from the "present" on the time line toward the signer.

Incorporating Numbers: Time Signs

Signs relating to time can also incorporate numbers, indicating more than one of whatever time unit the signer is using. For example:

Signs can move along the time line and incorporate numbers at the same time:

Repetition of Time Signs

Repeating time signs such as those in this lesson is one way to indicate that something is done on a regular basis.

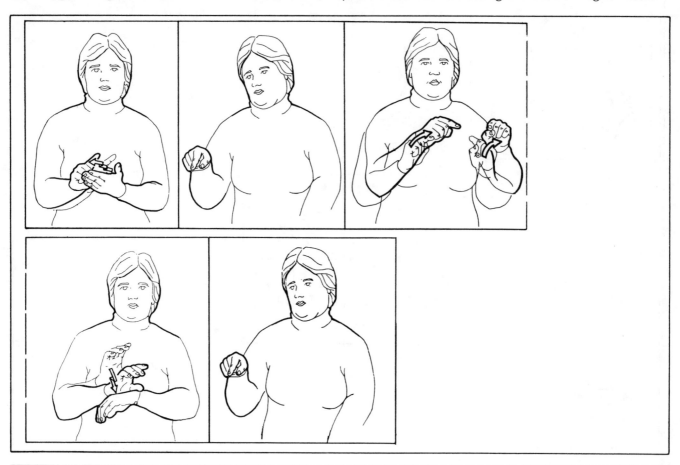

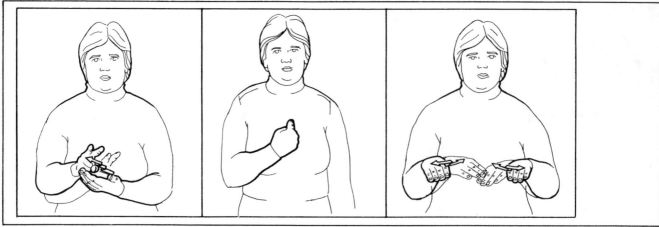

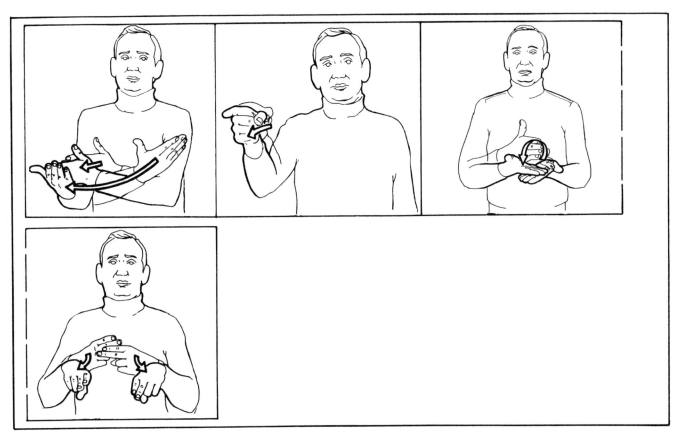

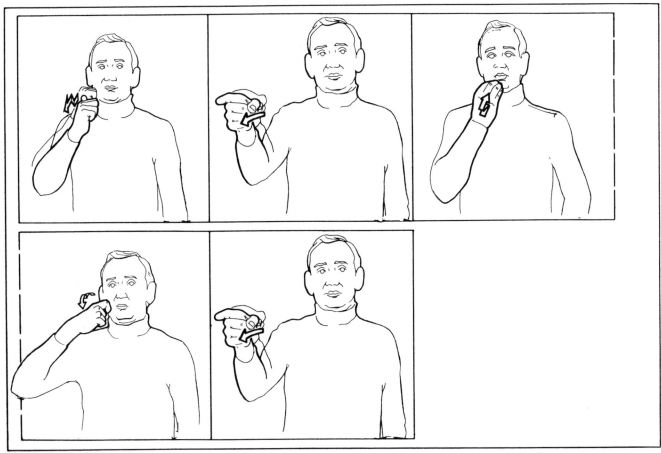

The closeness in time signal (see p. 31)
can also be used with these time signs.

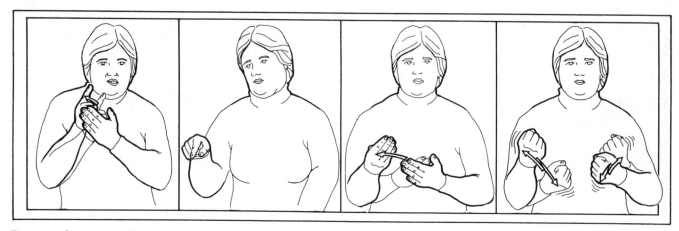

Practice the signs relating to time using the sentences already shown and the sentences below as models.

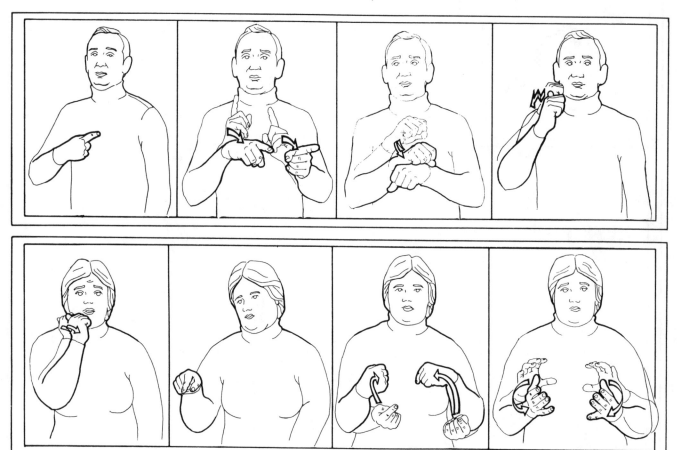

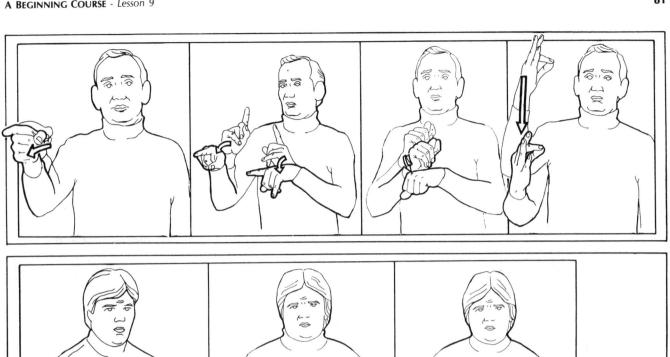

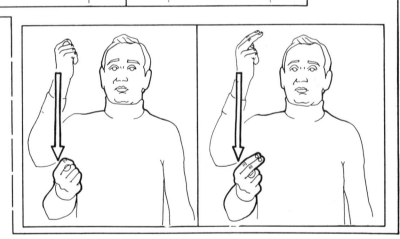

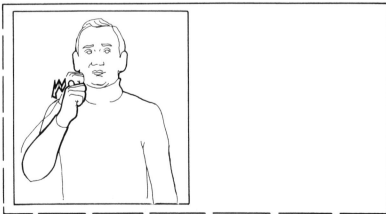

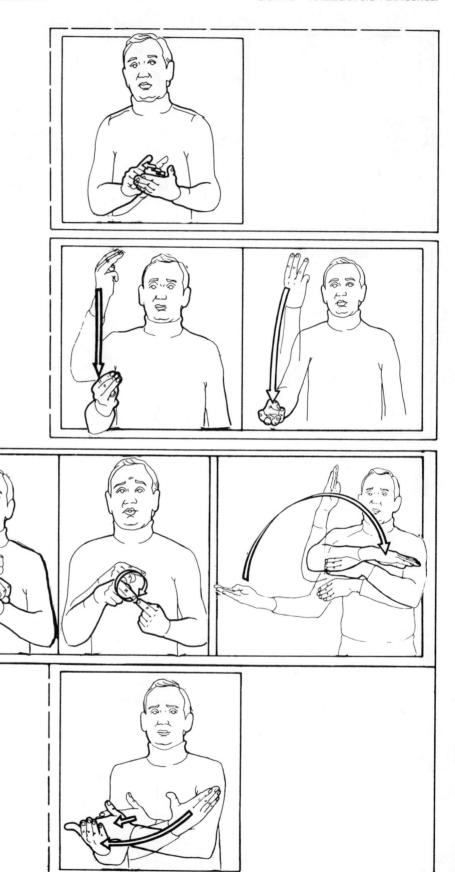

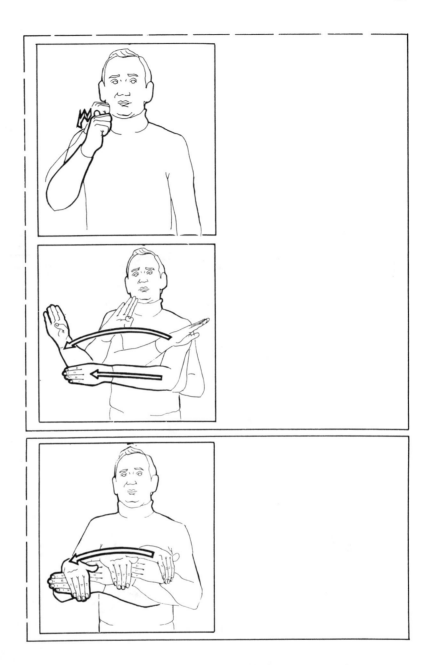

Inflecting Verbs: Regularity

In ASL many action verbs can be inflected to show that the action is done repeatedly or on a regular basis.

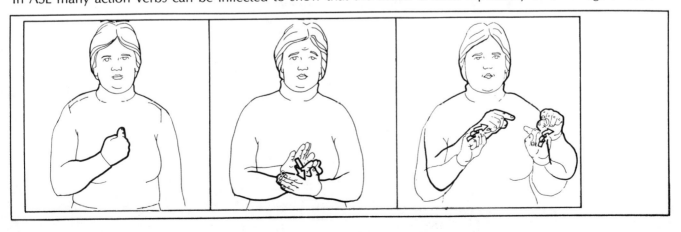

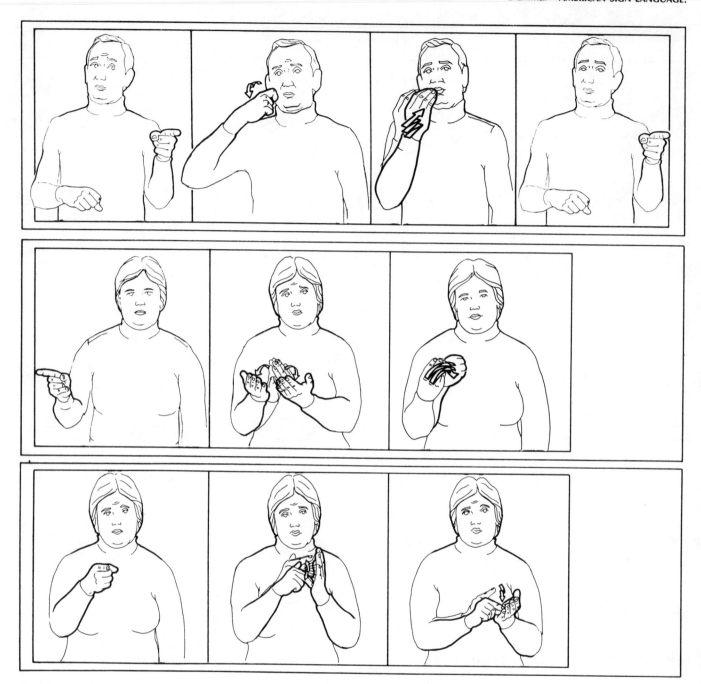

Practice this inflection using the sentences shown above as models.

Vocabulary

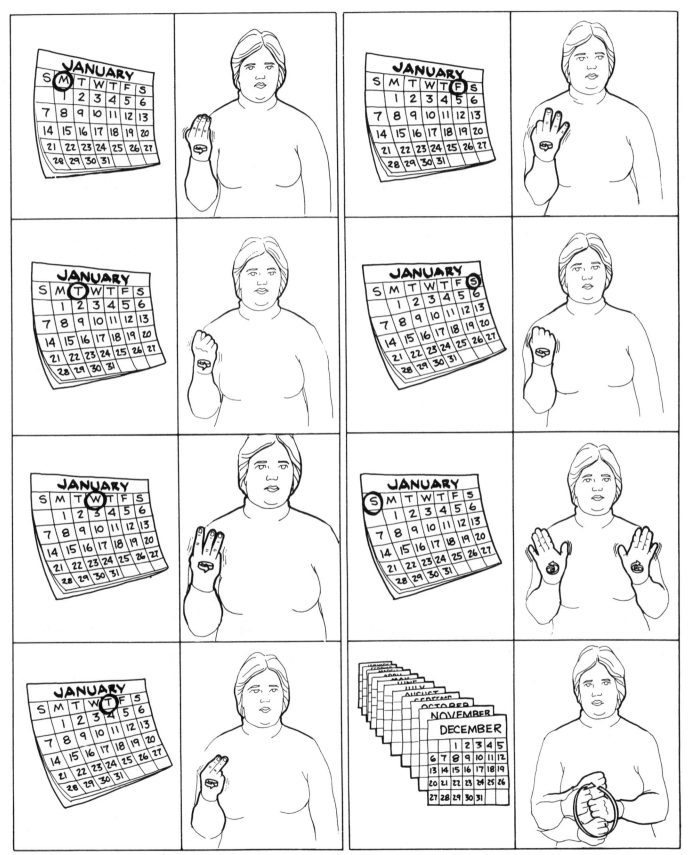

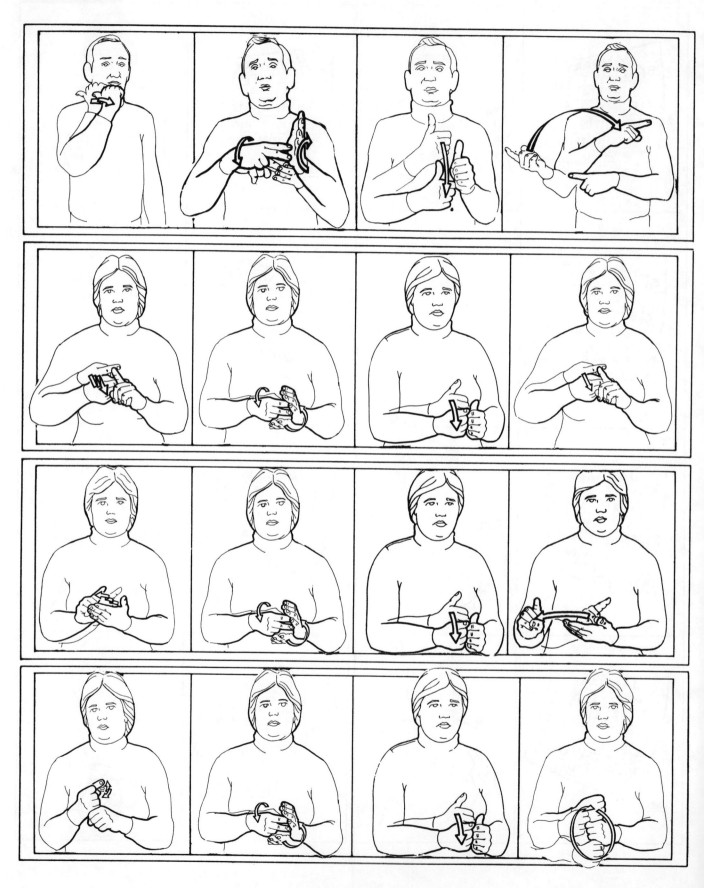

Definitions

Definitions (continued)

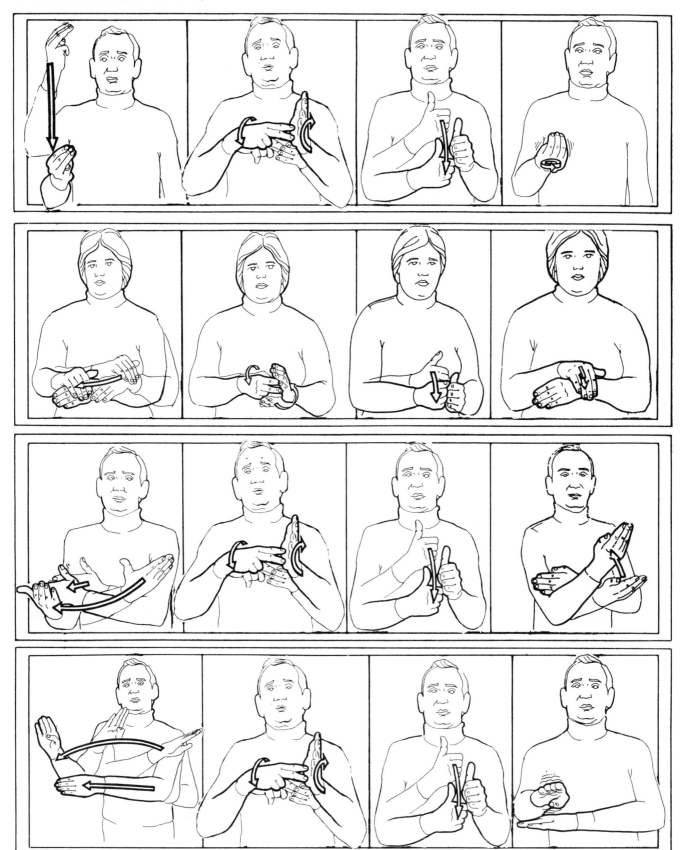

Comparative Conjunctions

In Lesson 6 a way of conjoining sentences in ASL was introduced. Another form of conjunction occurs when people are comparing one thing to another. In the following examples one item is placed on the right of the signer, and one on the left. Notice the topic signal as the signer sets up each, and notice how the signer uses eye gaze to help establish the referents.

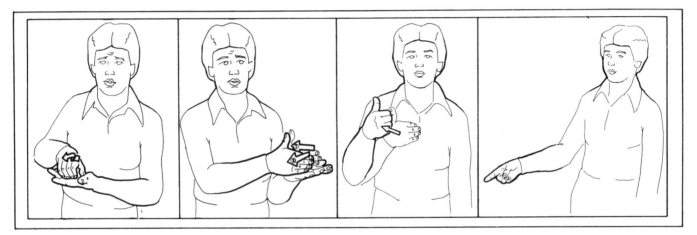

Pronominalization: Non-Present Referents

Lesson 3 discussed "real world" indexing of referents. In the example above, the two things are not present to the signer, but by setting them up in two different locations in space, they can then be referred to by pointing.

For signs that are made on or near the body (body-anchored signs) the signer must first make the sign, and then index it in space.

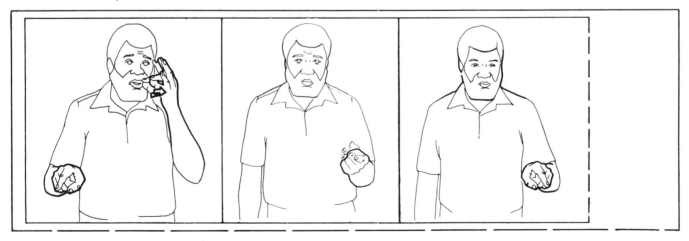

(Notice how the signer can use the non-dominant hand to index.)

Once a referent has been established in a certain location, that location will continue to stand for that referent, for both the signer and the addressee, until the signer moves it, or they change the subject of their conversation.

Practice making comparative conjunctions and indexing using the vocabulary you have learned so far and the sentences below as models.

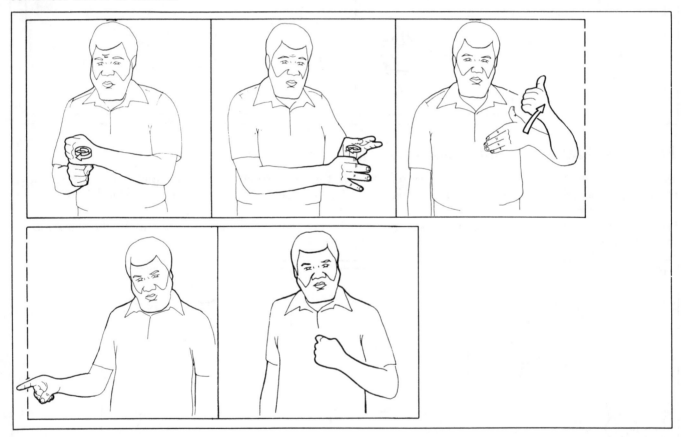

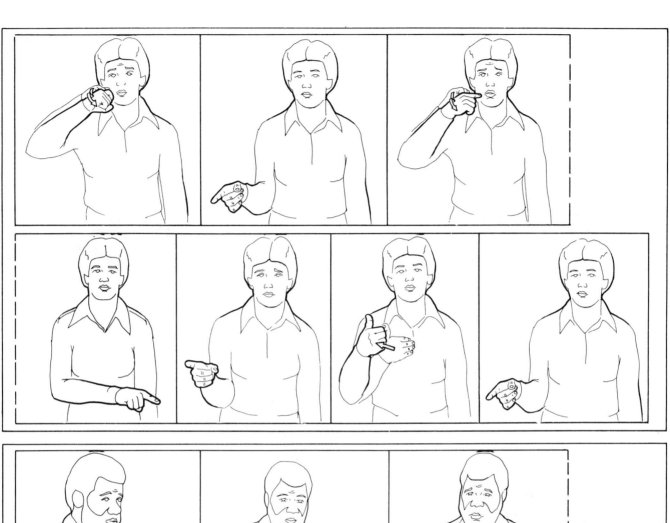

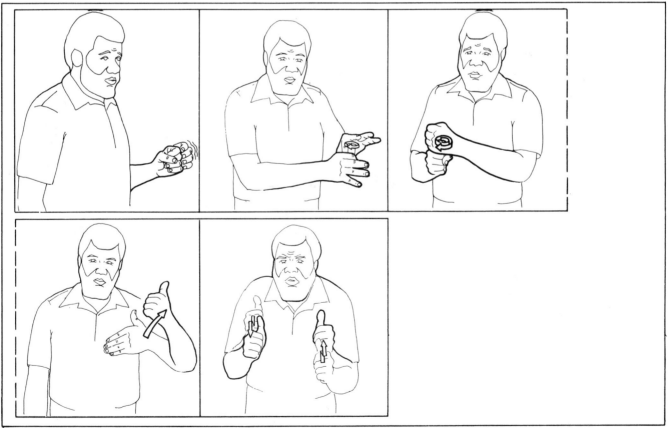

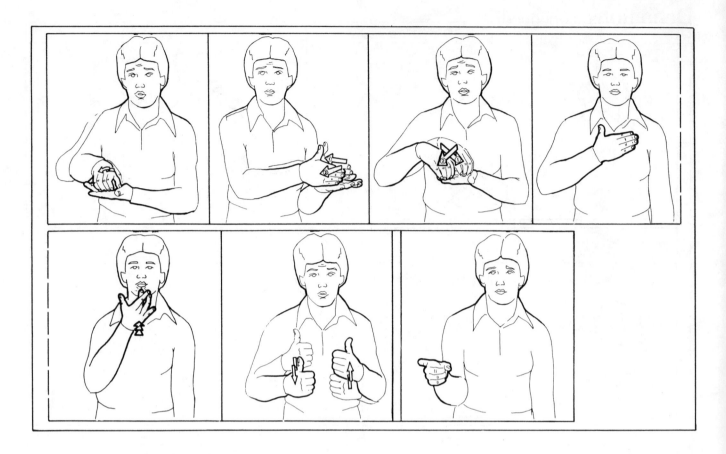

Verbs: Incorporation of Negation

In Lesson 3 you learned the sign

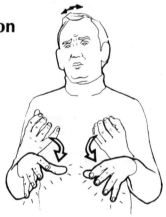

in which the negation was incorporated
into the movement of the sign.
Here is another sign

which can become its opposite by
incorporating negation into the
movement of the sign:

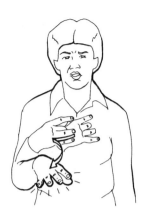

Vocabulary

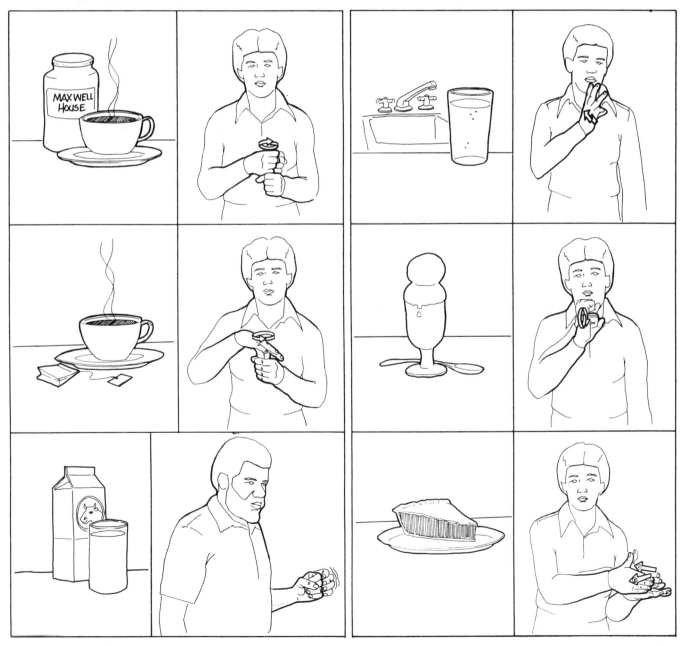

Vocabulary (continued)

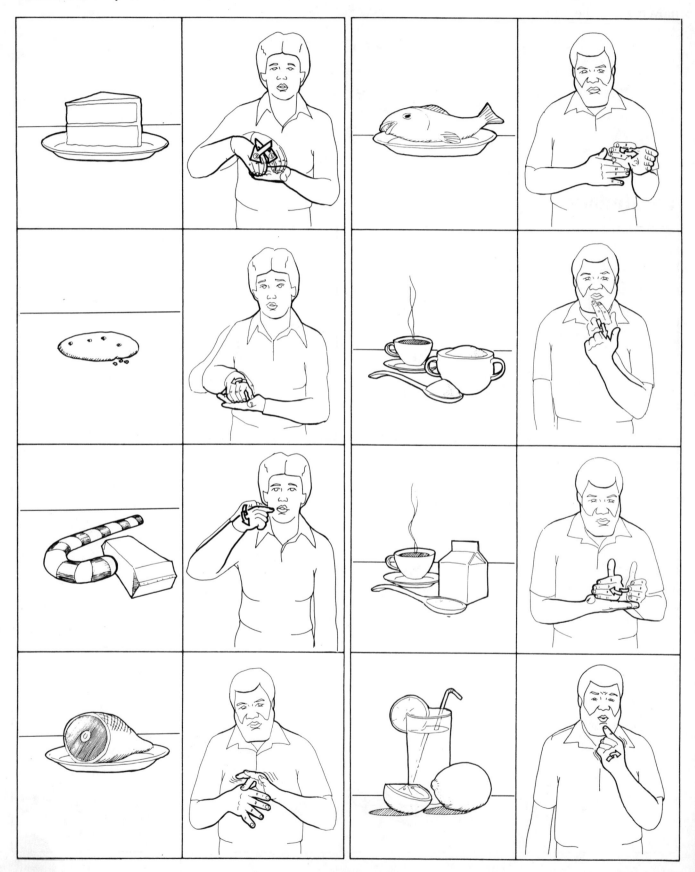

Vocabulary (continued)

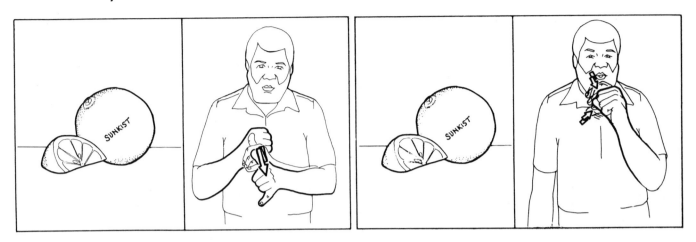

Definitions

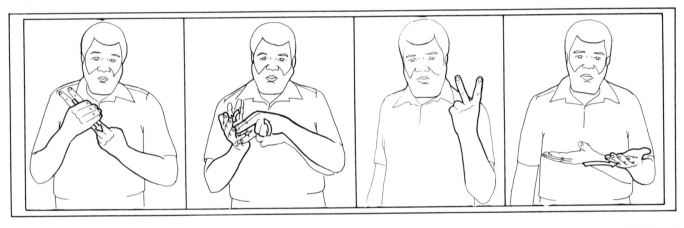

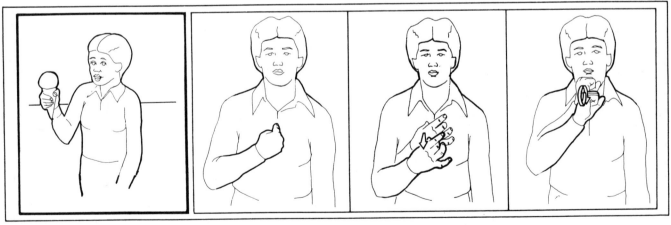

Definitions (continued)

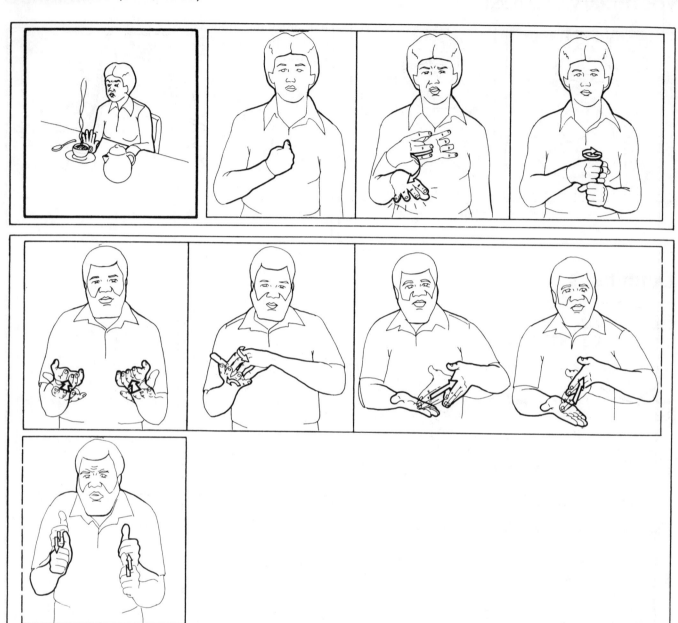

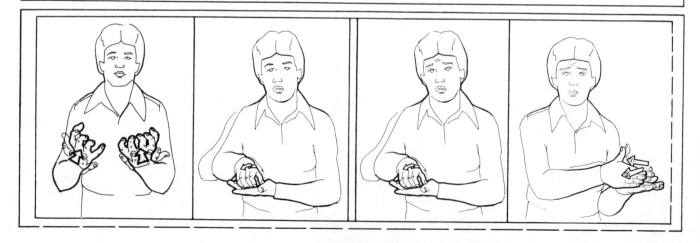

Definitions (continued)

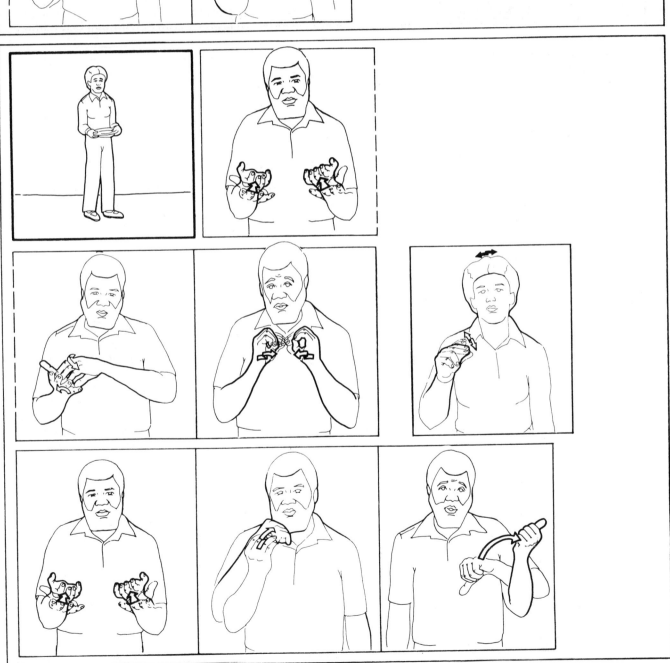

Definitions (continued)

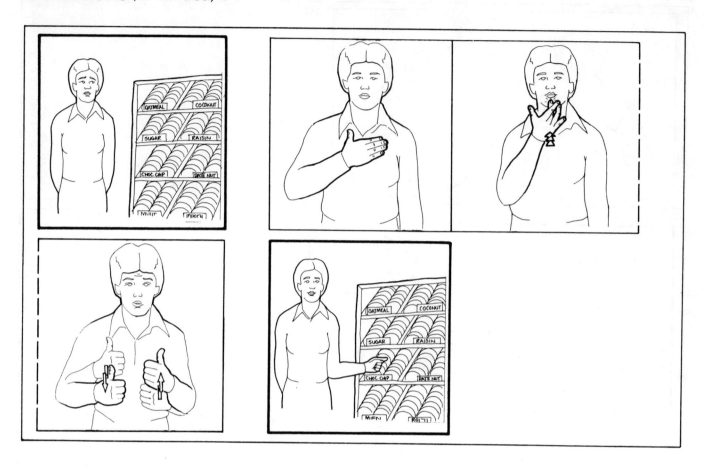

More Comparative Conjunctions

For comparing qualitative differences between people and things, the following conjunctions can be used:

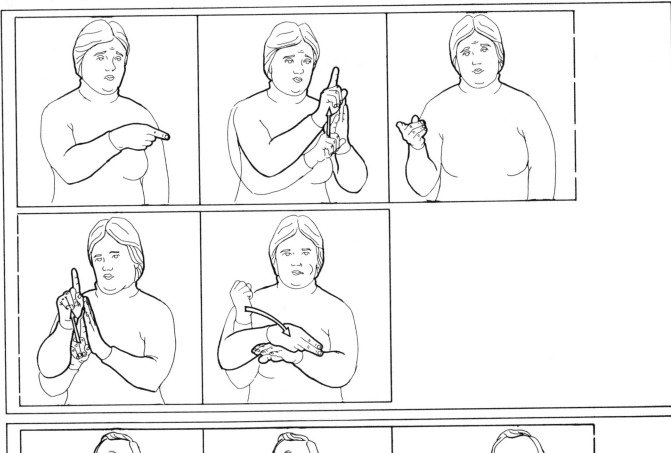

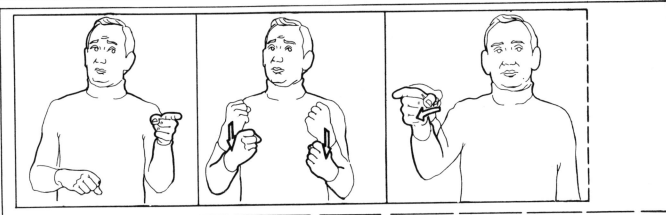

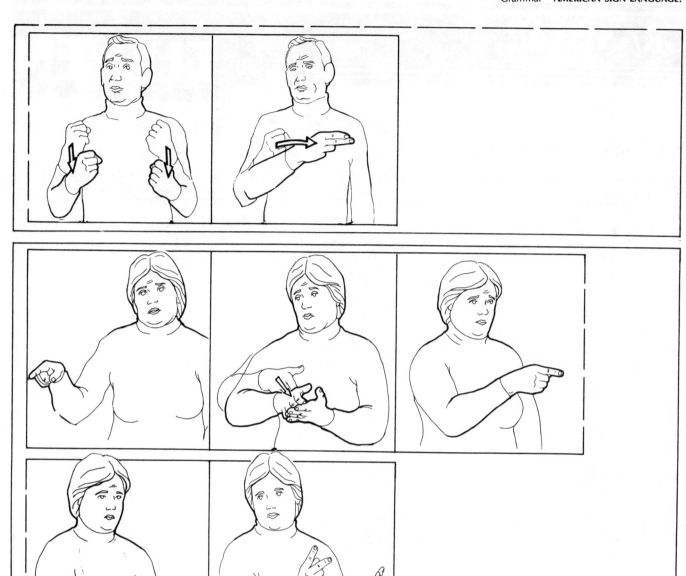

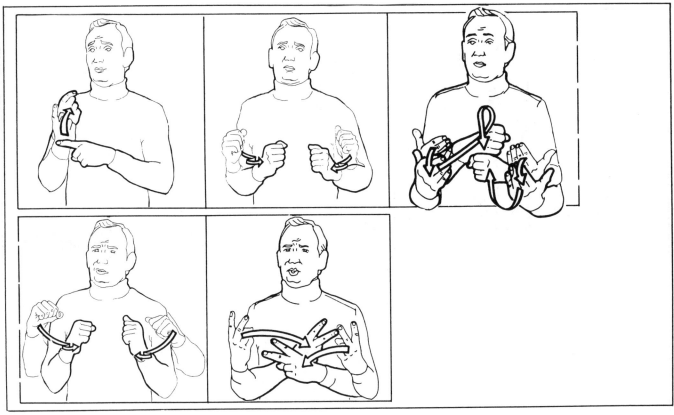

Superlatives

Superlatives are used when comparing more than two things. For example:

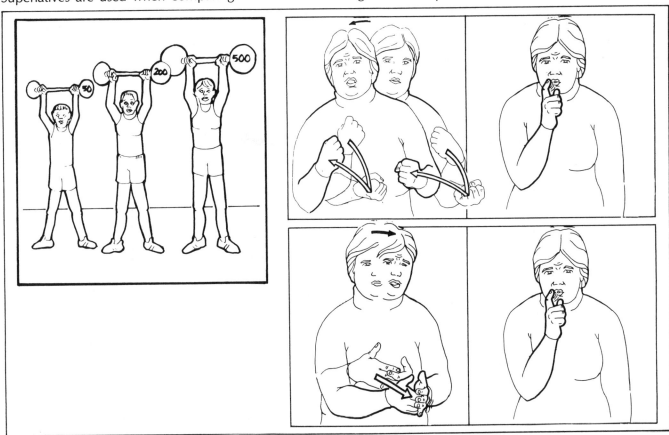

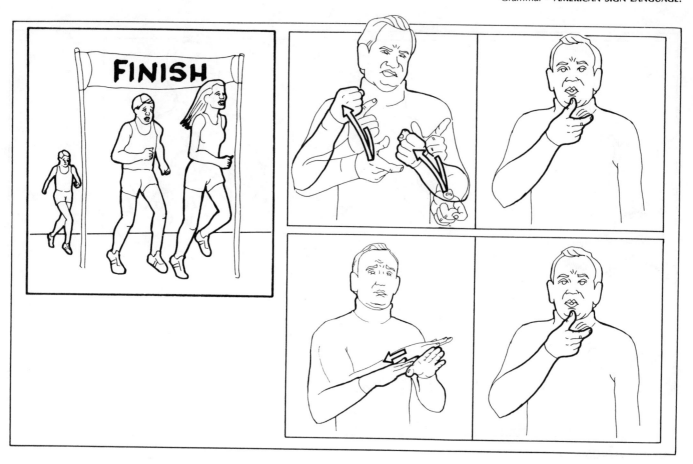

Lesson 4 introduced a non-manual grammatical signal (p. 26) that can be used with inflected verbs to show the degree of intensity of an action. The same signal can also be used with adjectives. In the drawings below and on the next page, Example 1 shows the adjective without the non-manual signal, and Example 2 shows the adjective with the non-manual signal.

Example 1   ## Example 2

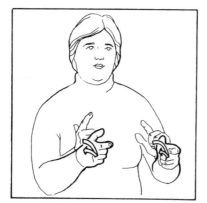

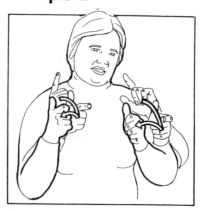

Example 1   ## Example 2

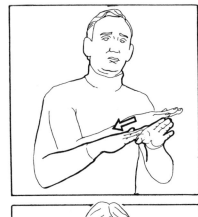 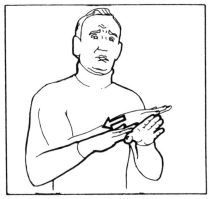

 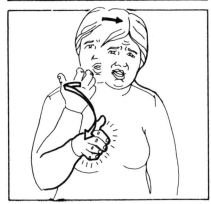

Practice this signal by taking the simple statements below and intensifying them.

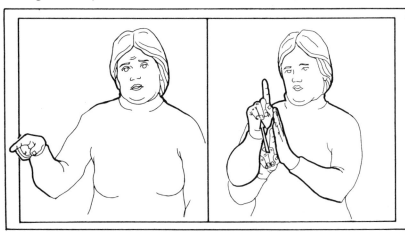

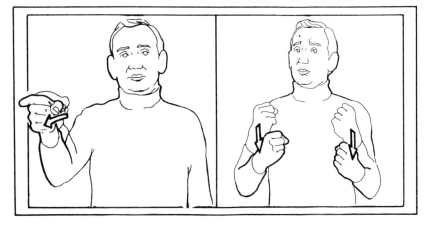

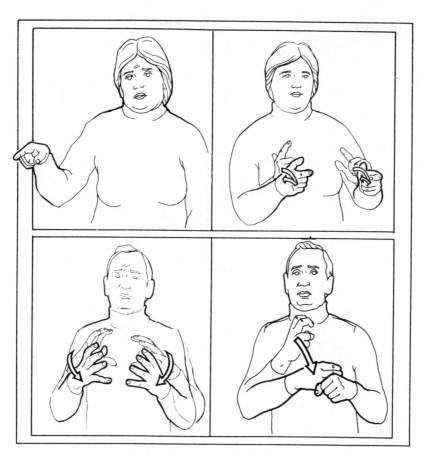

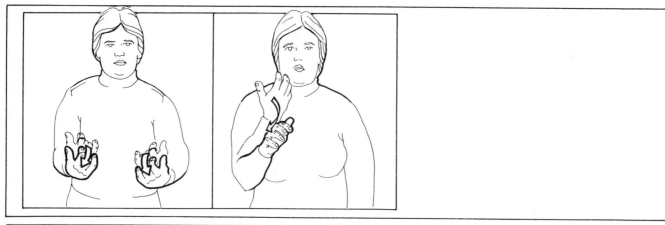

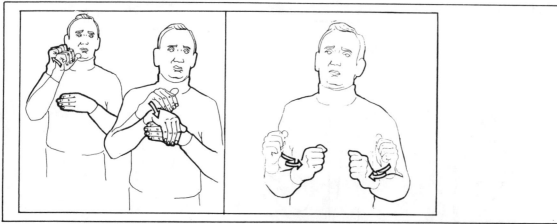

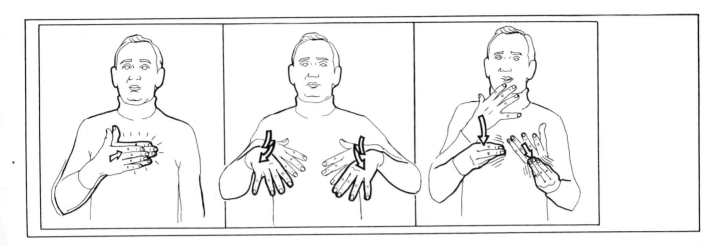

Vocabulary

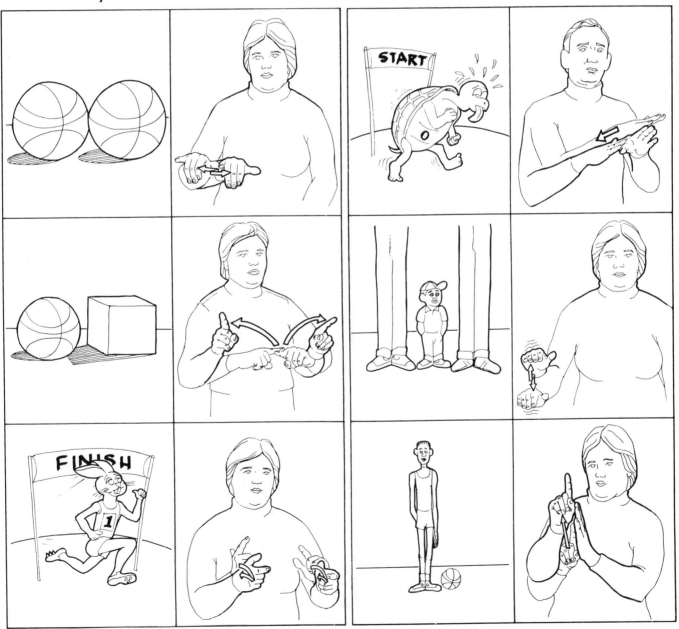

Vocabulary (continued)

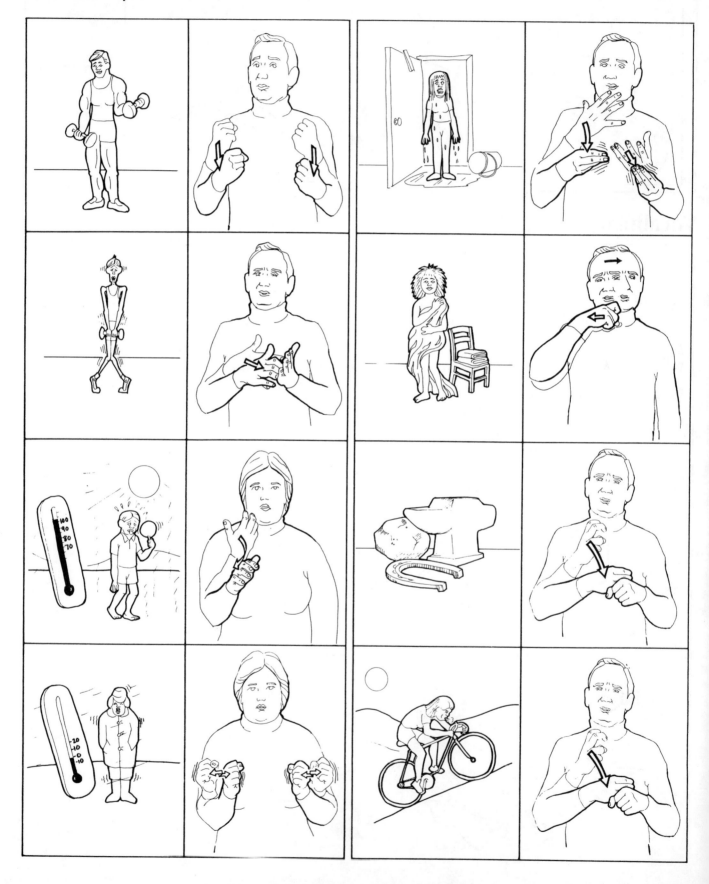

Vocabulary (continued)

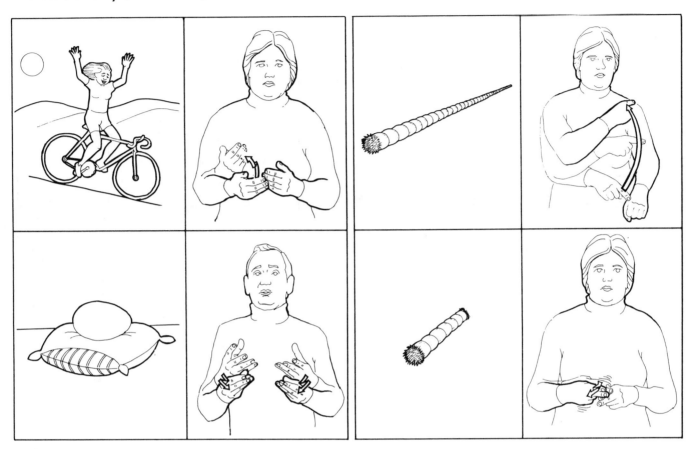

Definitions

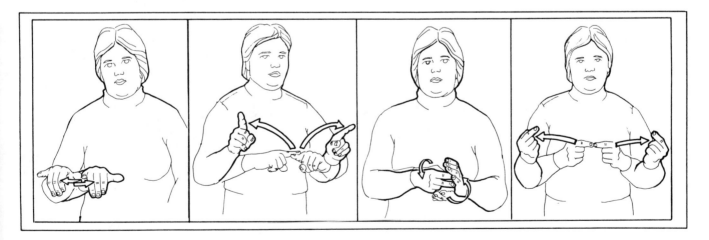

Definitions (continued)

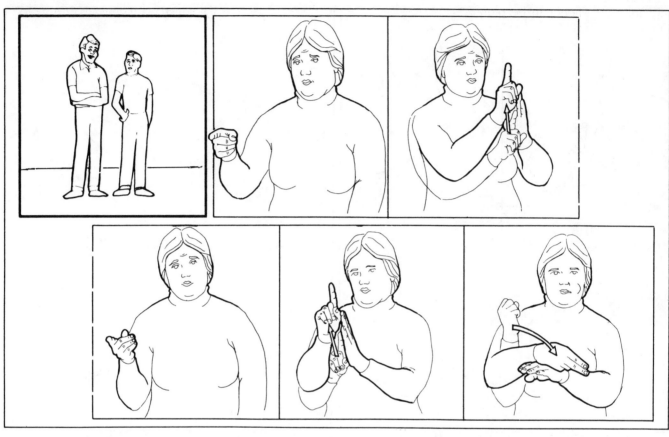

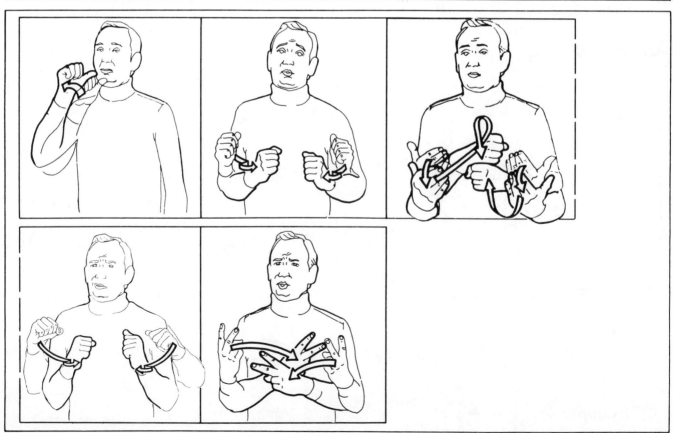

Pronominalization

Another pronoun in ASL is:

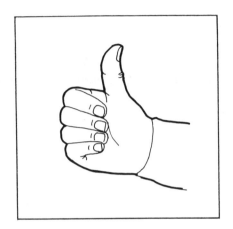

It can function in two ways. It can be reflexive:

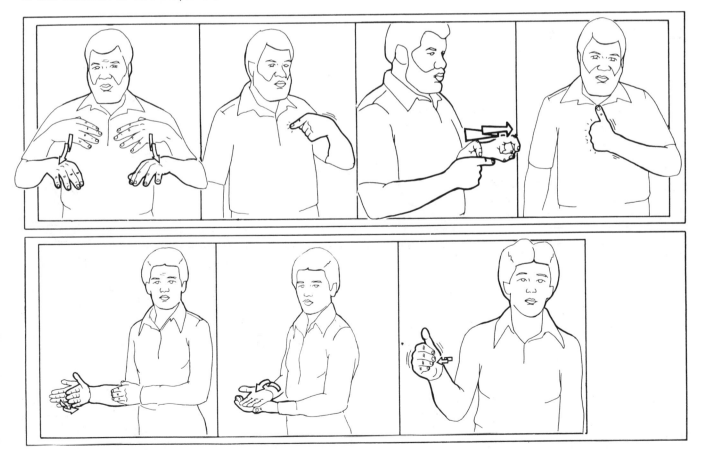

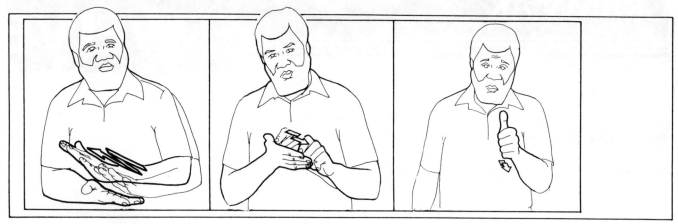

The second way this handshape can be used is as a personal pronoun, much in the way we have already seen. (The first two examples are singular, the third is plural.)

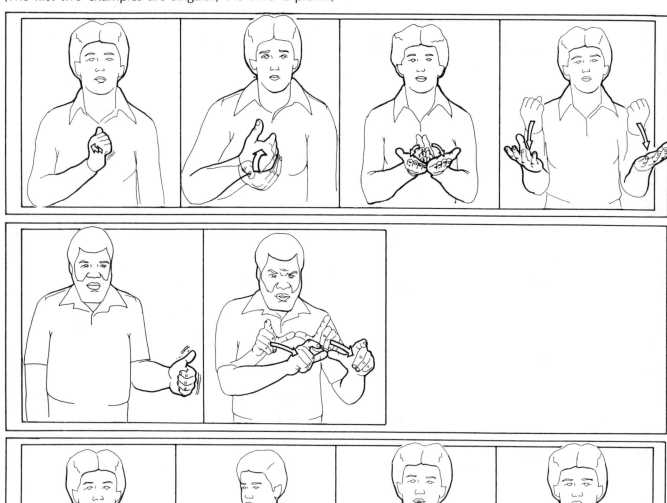

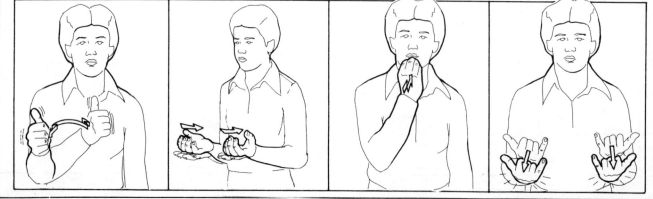

Inflection of Verbs: Continuous Action

Another inflection that some verbs can take is one which shows that an action is or was done continuously. For example:

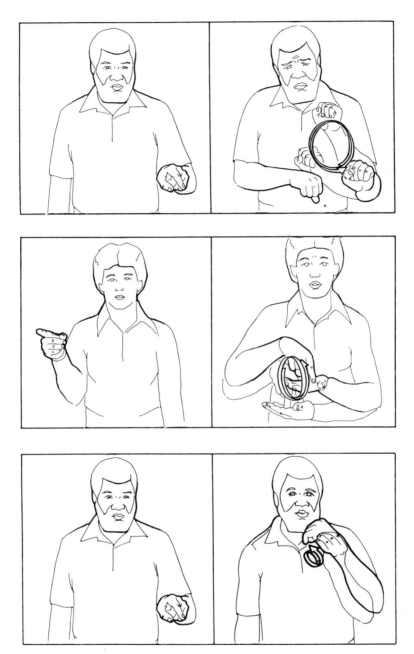

Notice the difference between the inflection for continuous action and the inflection for repetition or regularity.

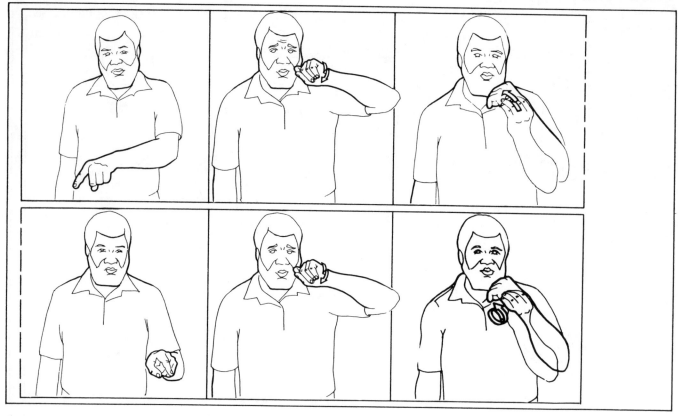

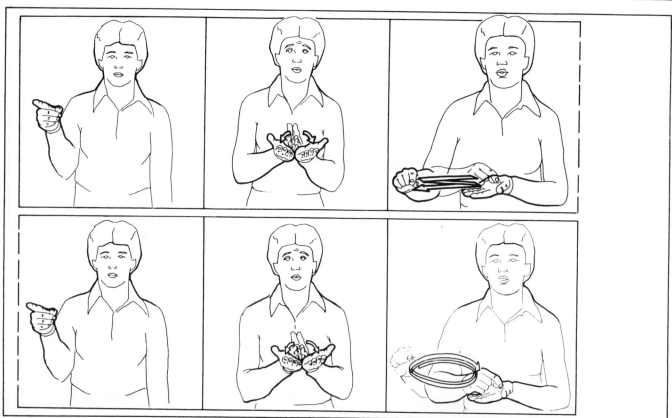

Four Non-Manual Grammatical Signals Used With Verbs

In Lesson 4 we saw that many action verbs can be inflected to show how something is done. ASL also has certain non-manual grammatical signals that can be used with action verbs and which give specific adverbial information.

Here are some more non-manual grammatical signals that can be used with many action verbs to give information on how the action was done.

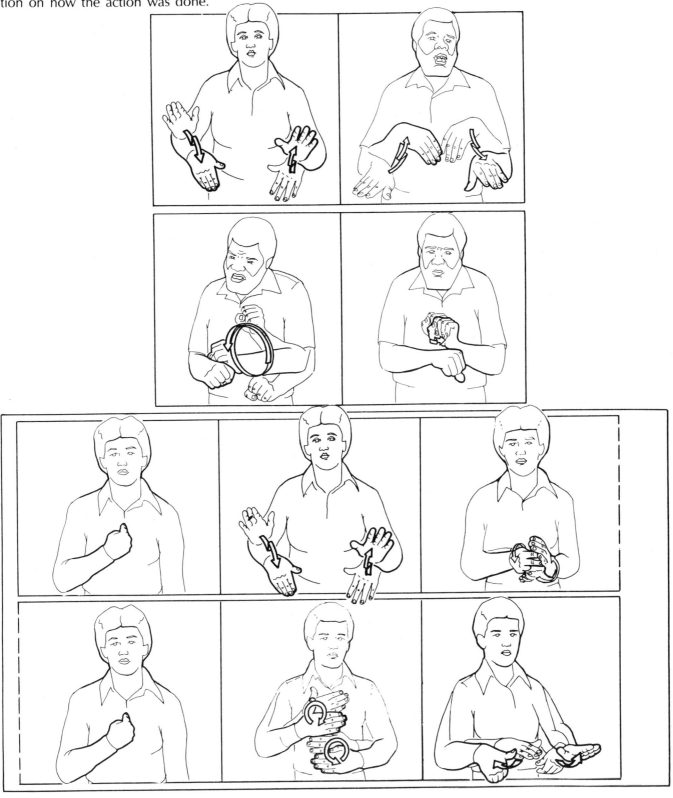

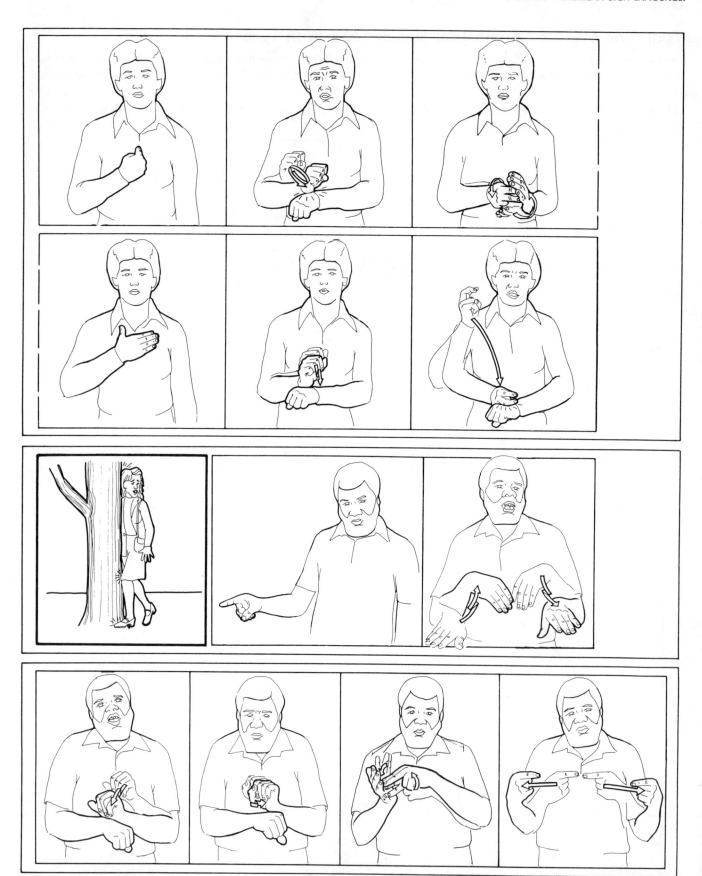

Practice these non-manual signals and the inflections in this lesson using the sentences below as models.

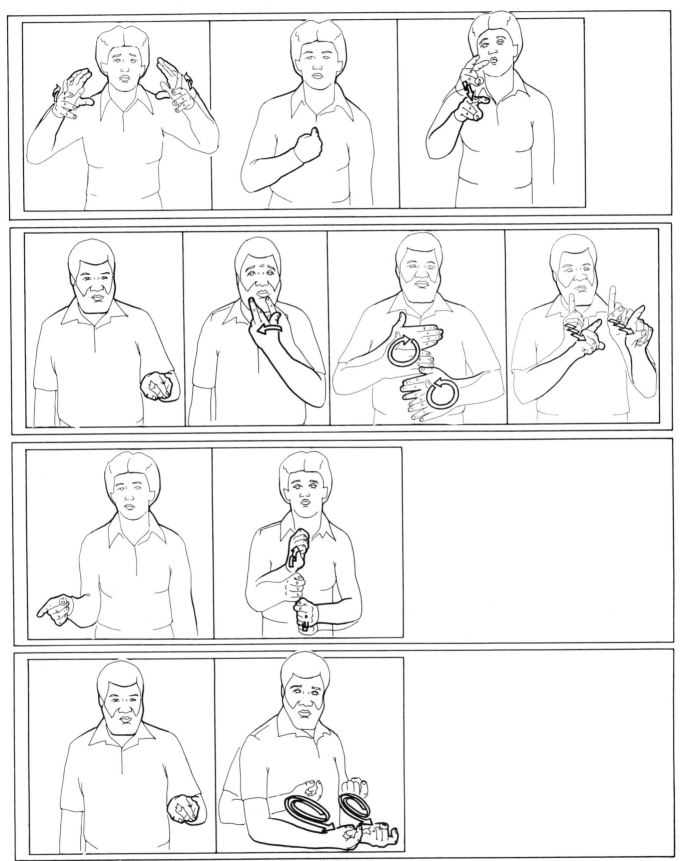

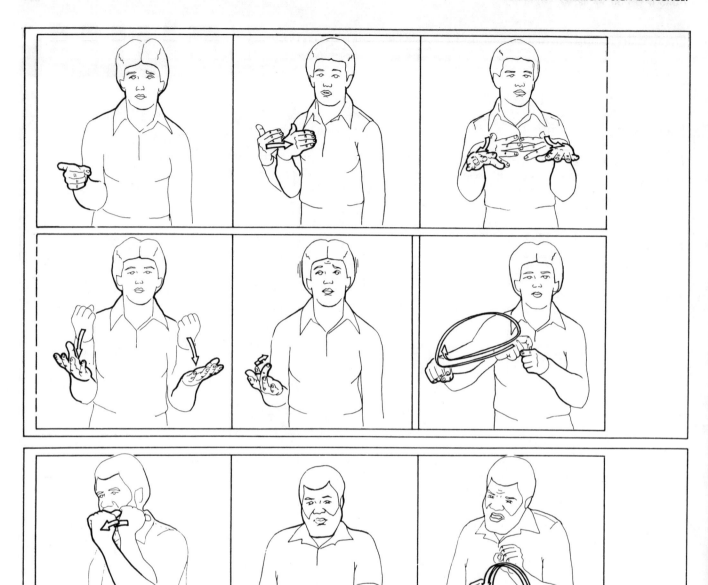

Vocabulary

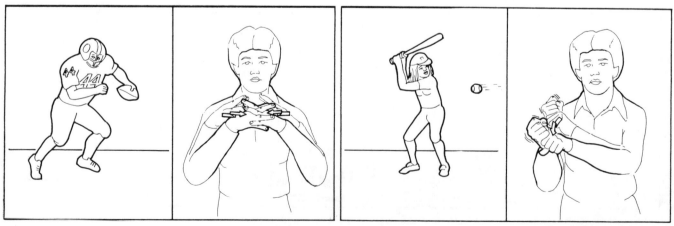

Vocabulary (continued)

Vocabulary (continued)

Definitions

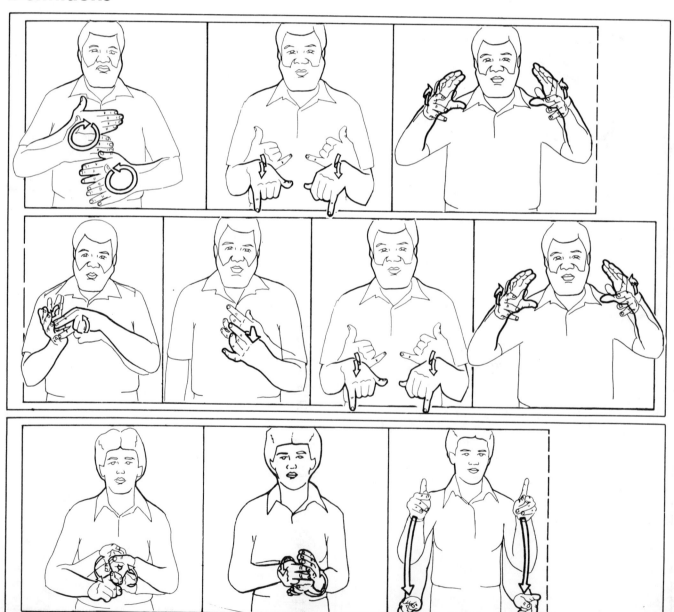

Definitions (continued)

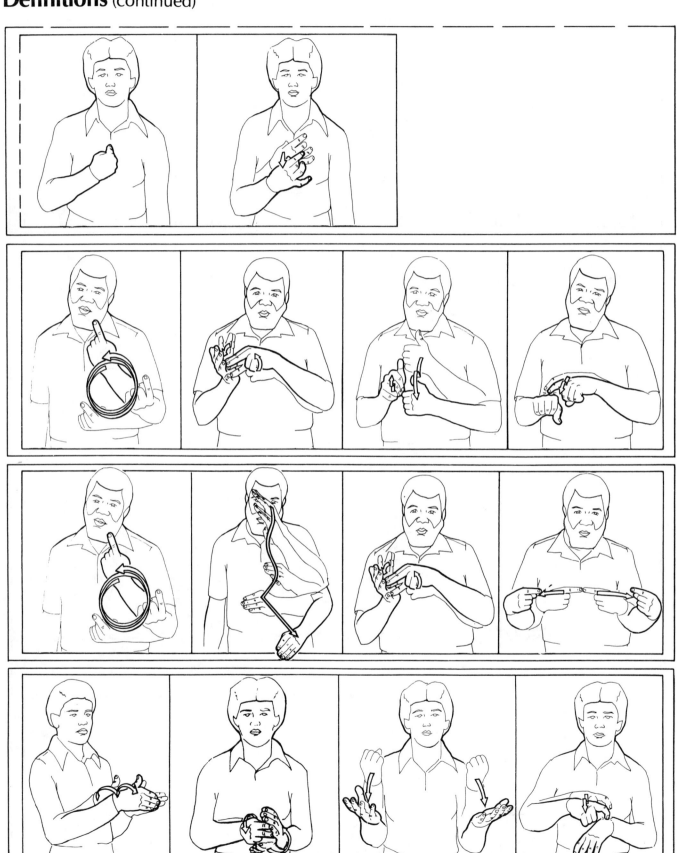

Definitions (continued)

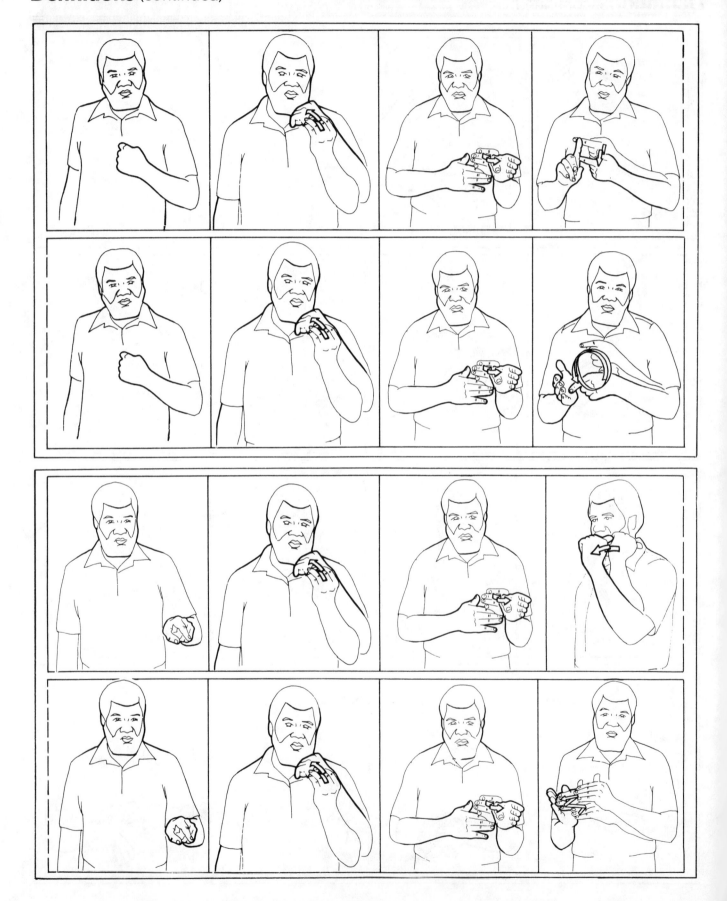

Noun/Verb Pairs

These classifiers are pronouns because they can stand for any of the nouns in the category of things they represent. Because they are pronouns, they must be identified before being used.

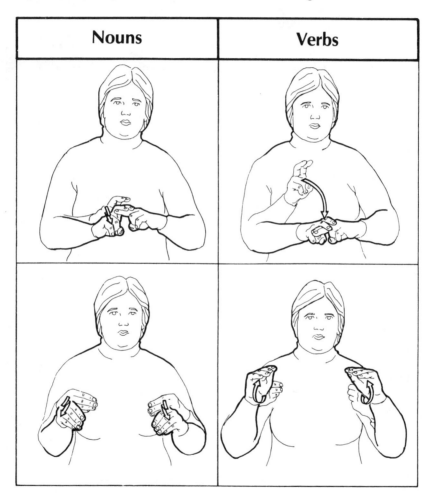

Nouns	Verbs

Nouns (continued)	**Verbs** (continued)

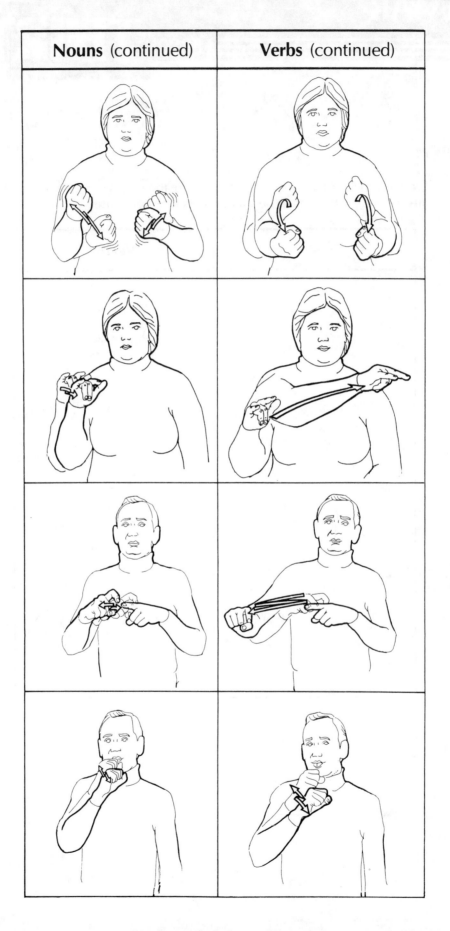

Nouns (continued)	**Verbs** (continued)
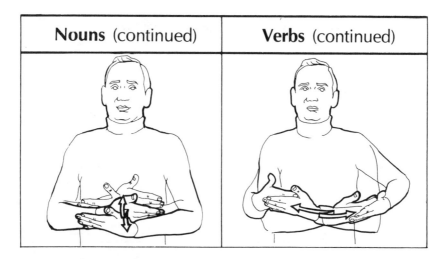	

The movement for the nouns in these examples is repeated and is much shorter than the movement for the verbs. The movement for verbs can be one continuous motion or a continuous repeated motion.

Classifiers

Classifiers are signs that represent groups or classes of things. Here are some examples:

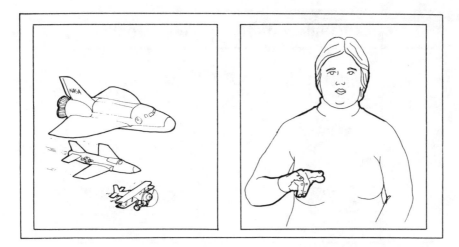

These classifiers are pronouns because they can stand for any of the nouns in the category of things they represent. Because they are pronouns, they must be identified before being used.

These classifiers can also act as verbs because they can be moved to show the action of what they are representing.

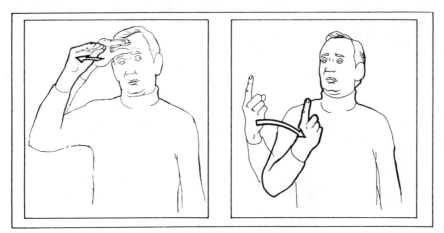

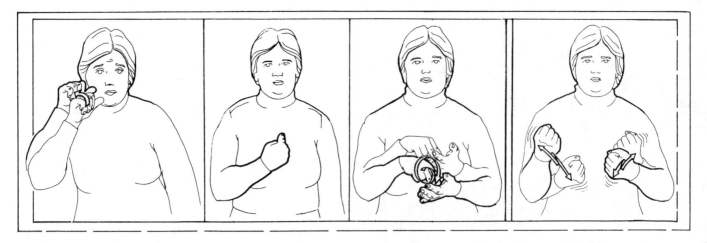

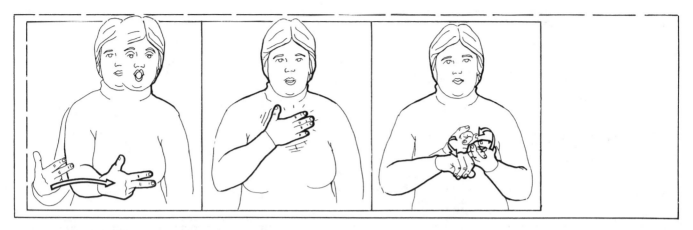

Verbs That Help Establish Location

Some verbs, by the way they are moved, show the way referents moved and help establish a relation between 'here' and 'there'. For example:

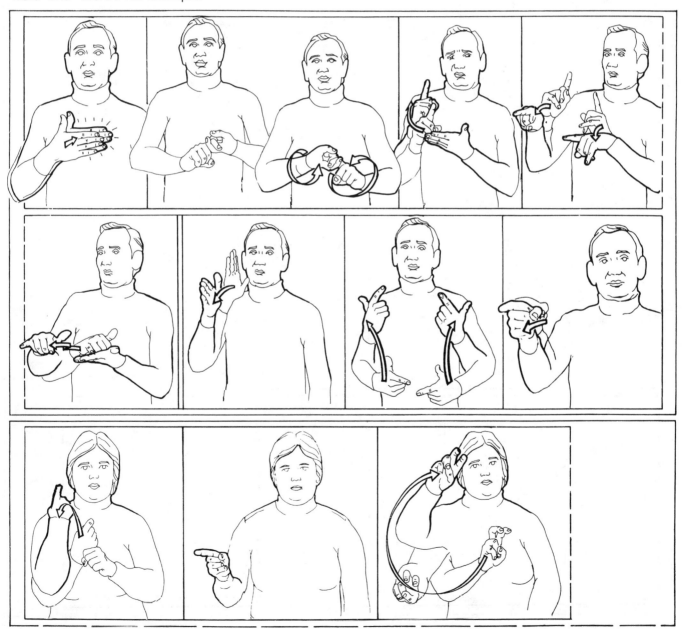

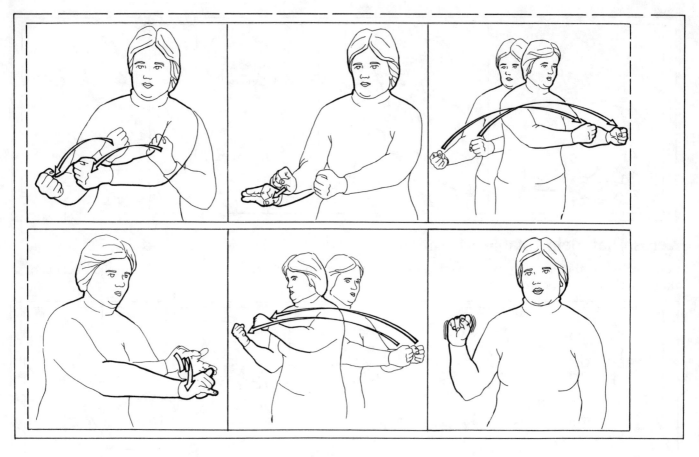

Conjunctions

The sign 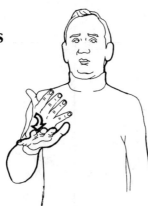 which can establish past tense can also function as a conjunction.

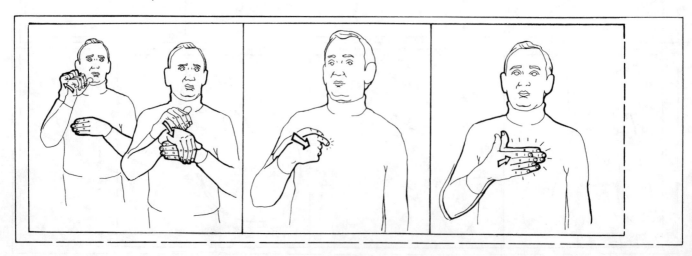

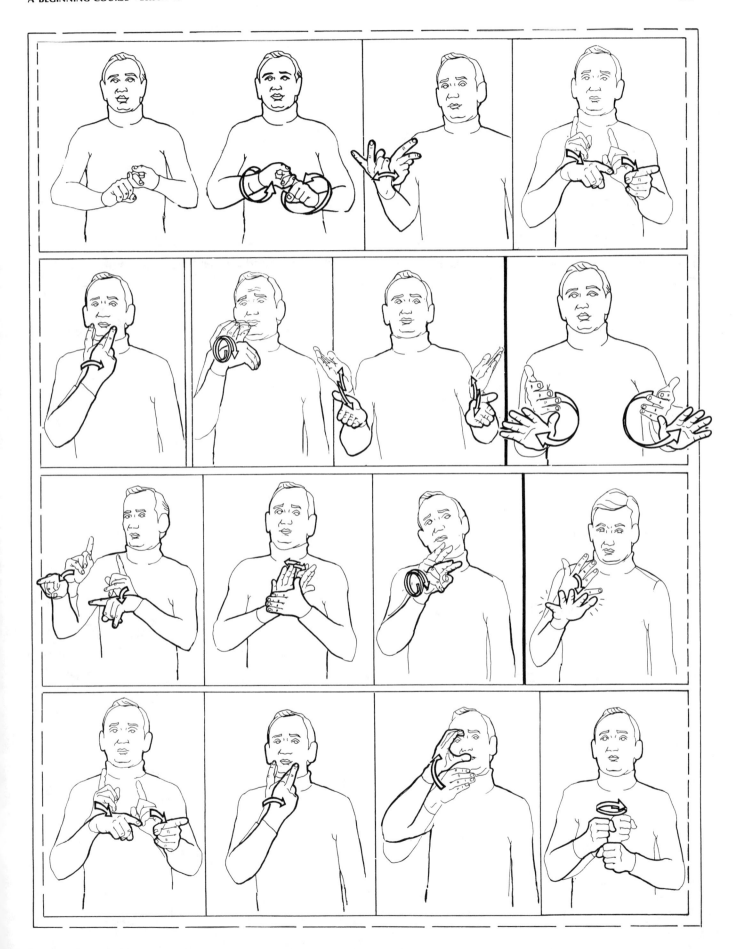

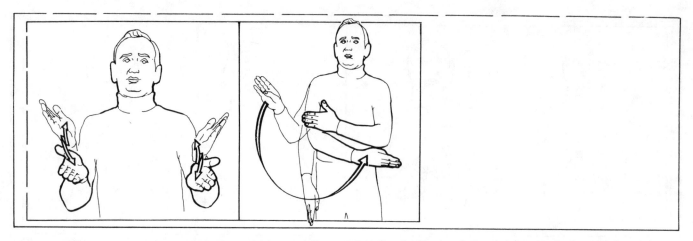

Practice the grammar in this lesson using the sentences already shown and the sentences below as models.

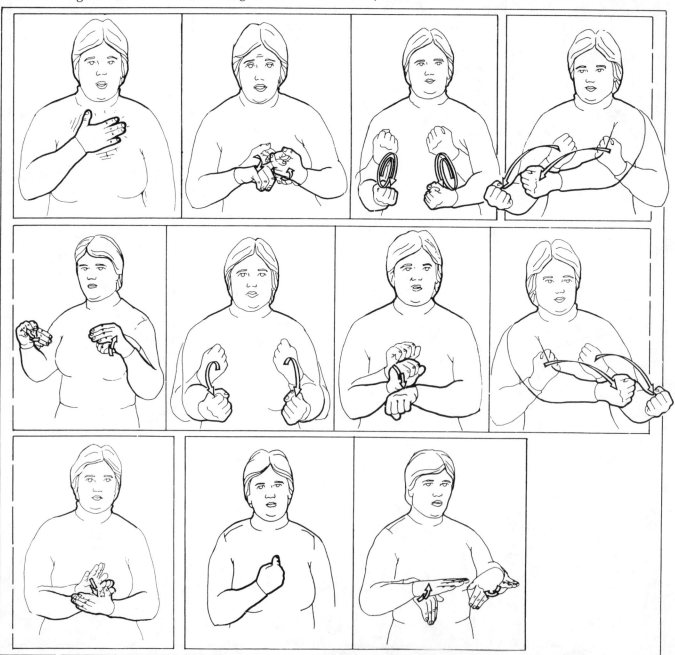

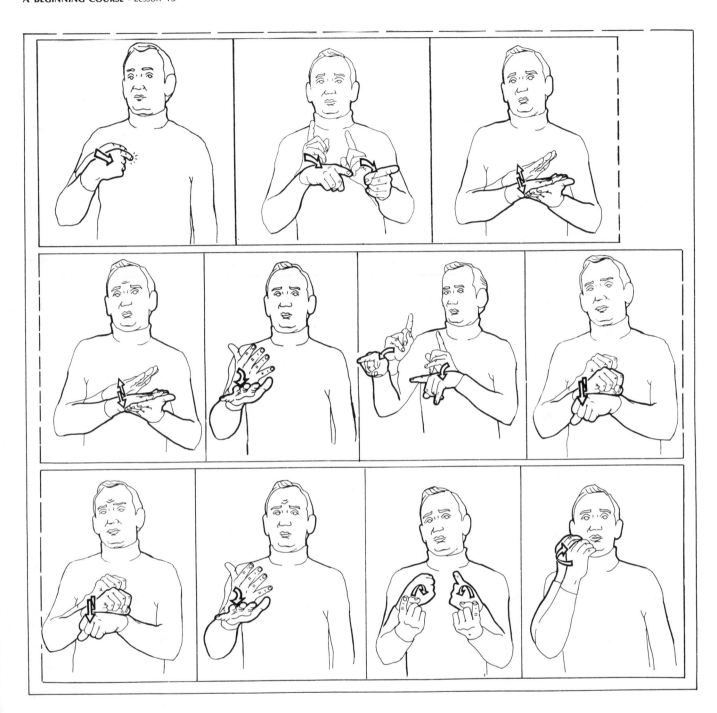

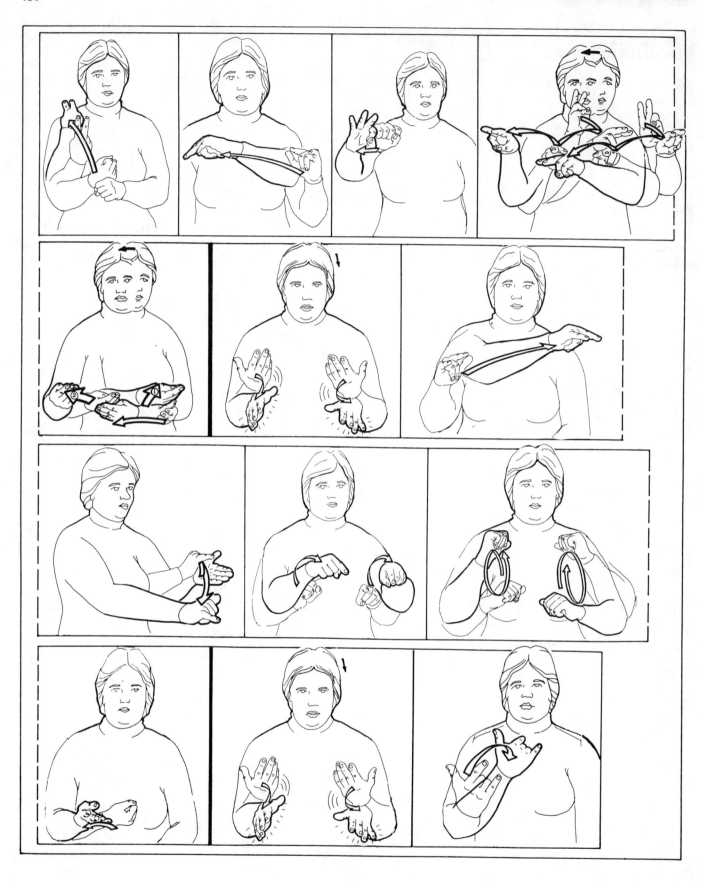

Vocabulary

Vocabulary (continued)

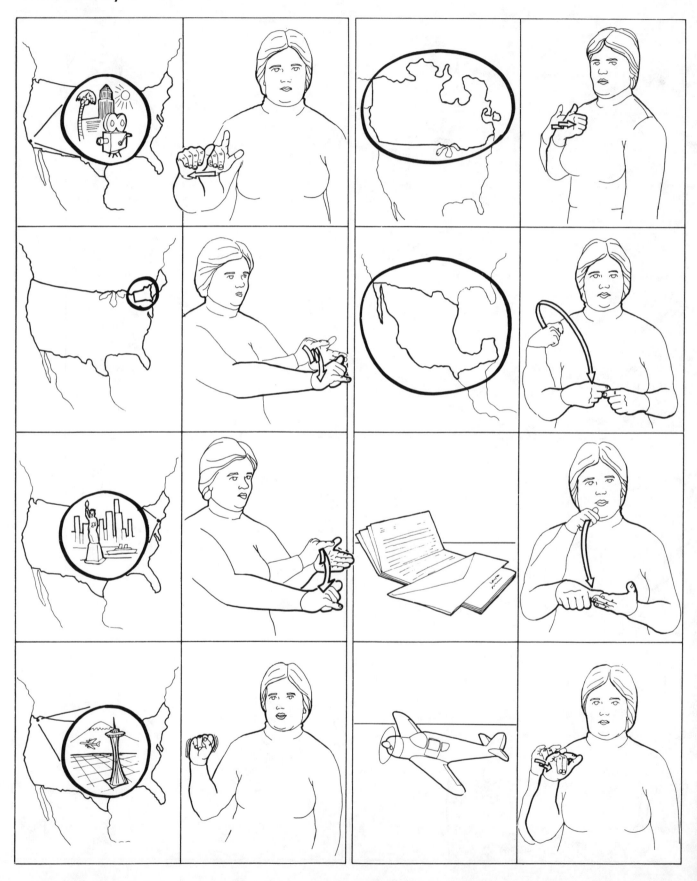

Vocabulary (continued)

Definitions

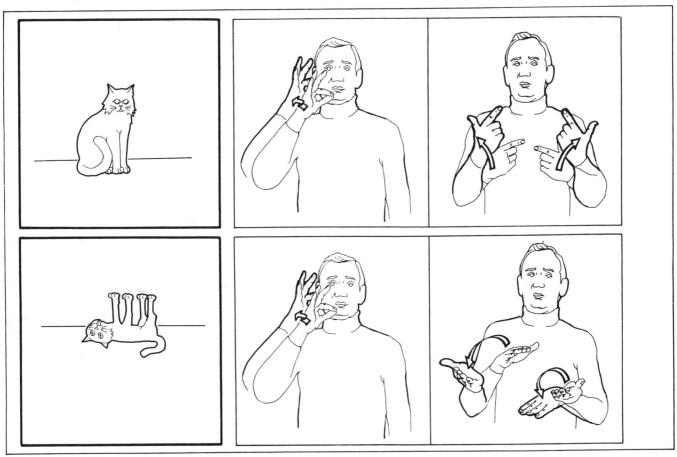

Definitions (continued)

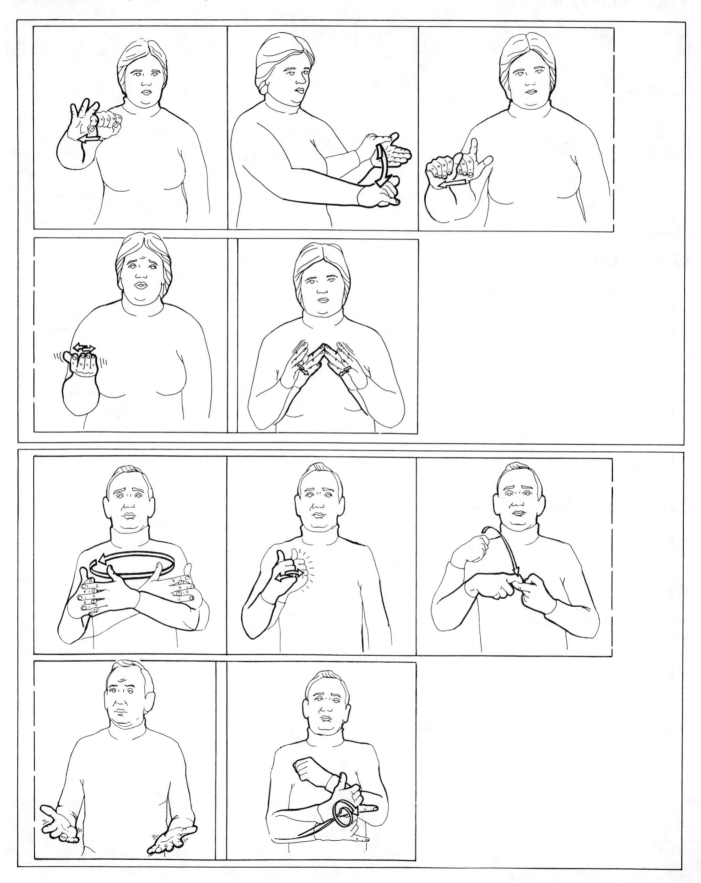

Definitions (continued)

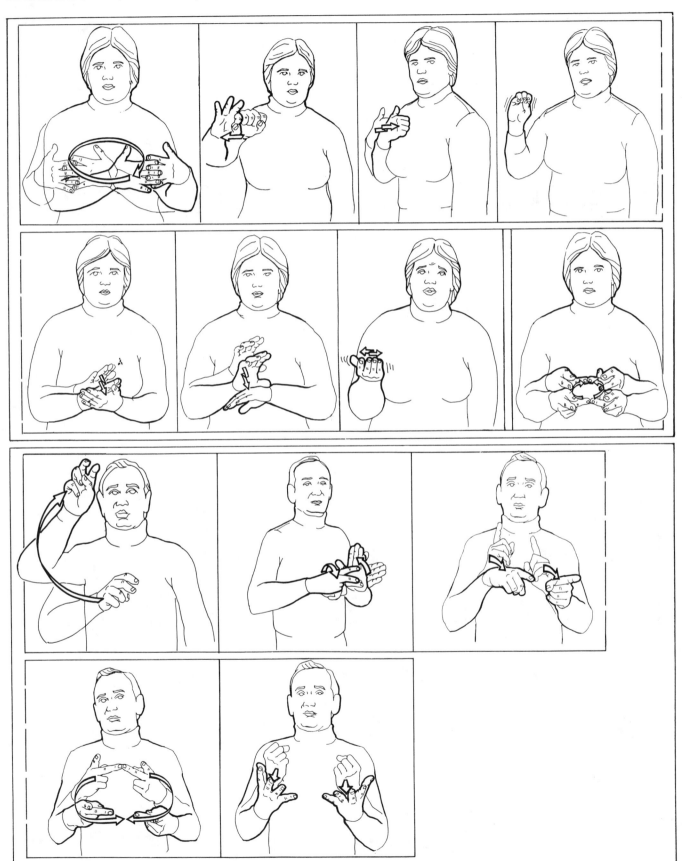

Definitions (continued)

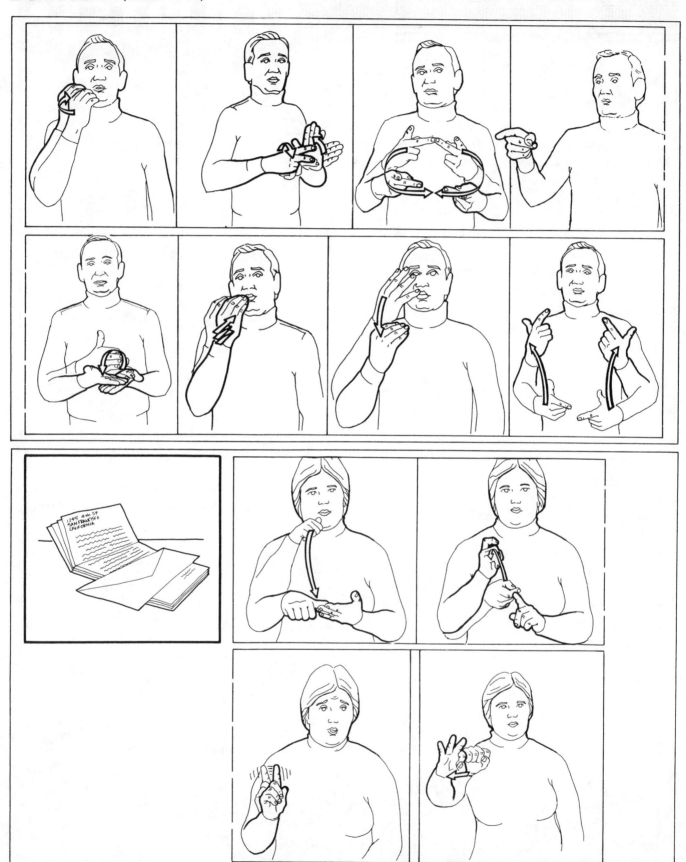

More Classifiers

Here are three more classifiers:

Classifiers as Verbs

The classifier in the first example if moved

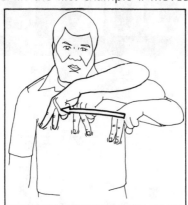

can represent

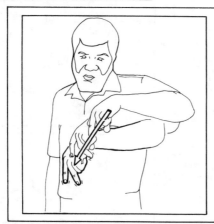

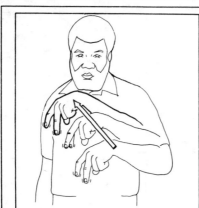

Classifiers as Prepositions

Classifiers can show the relation of things to one another and thus function as prepositions. For example:

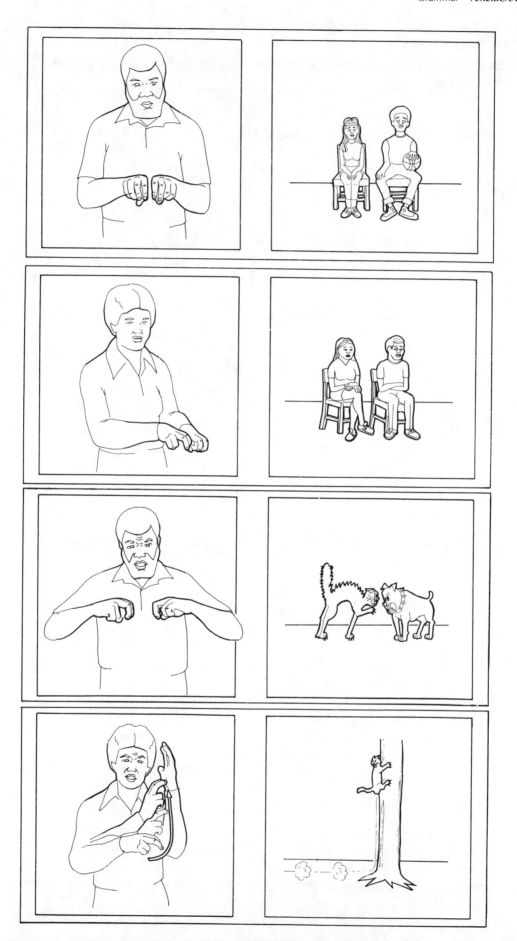

In the last examples, the classifier can be seen functioning as a pronoun, a verb, and a preposition at the same time. same time.

Using classifiers from this lesson and the last, show the relationships of the people, animals and things in the pictures below. If there is movement, show it also.

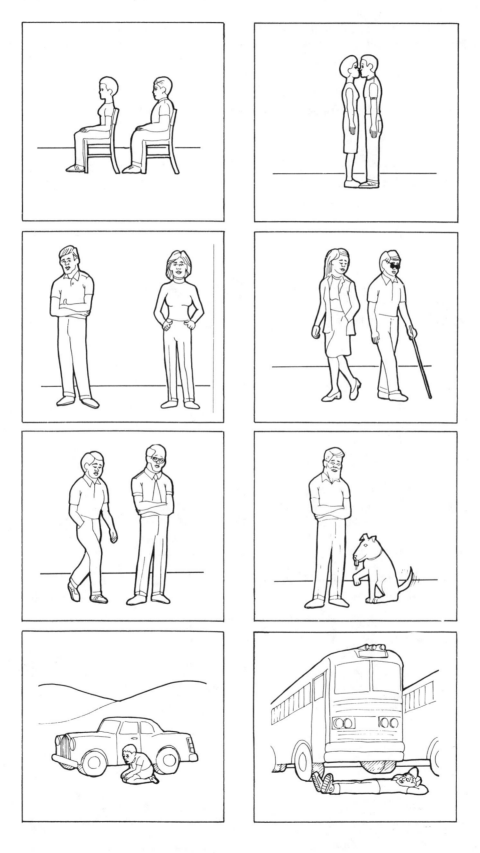

CULTURE

Name Signs

Many Deaf people, and hearing people who are involved in the Deaf Community, have name signs—signs given to them by parents or friends, or signs they invented for themselves. Name signs are often used because they are easier than fingerspelling people's names. In fact, if the name sign is based on a physical characteristic of that person, or some activity she habitually does, it can be more descriptive of her than her given name. Often a name sign will include the first letter of a person's name, but it never represents one particular name. Four boys named Tom, for example, will probably have four different name signs—if they have name signs at all. Some Deaf people prefer to spell their names, rather than have name signs.

Vocabulary

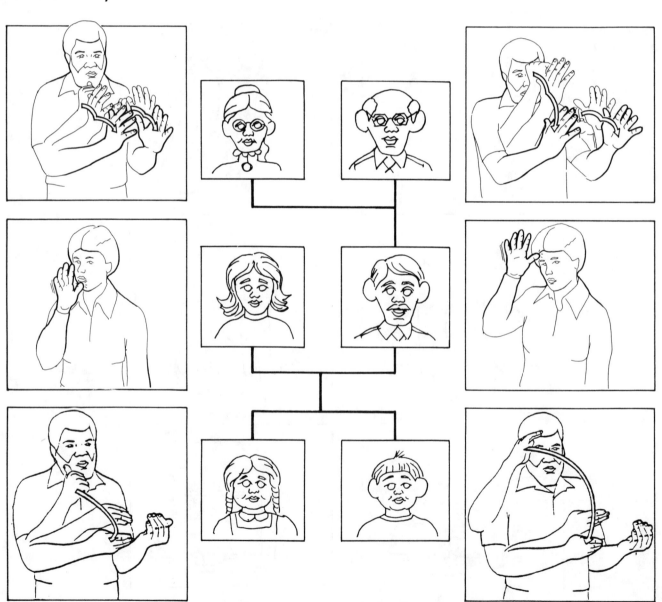

Vocabulary (continued)

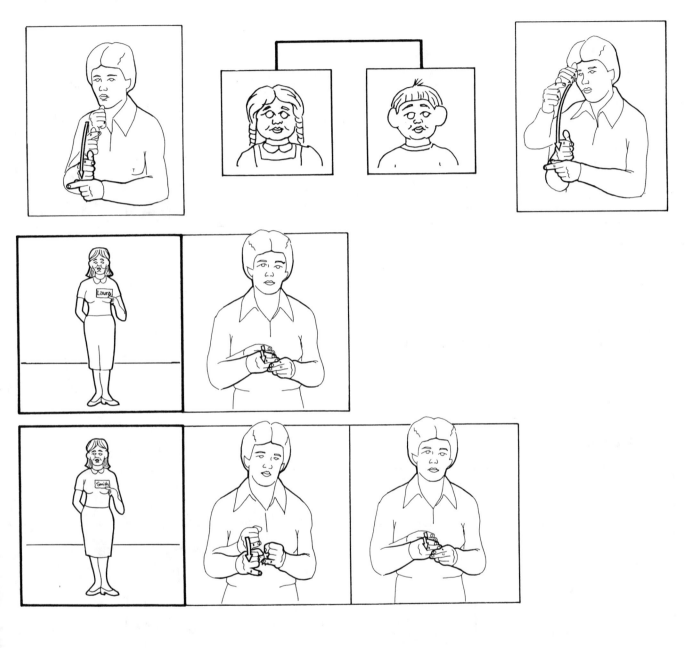

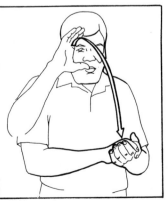

Vocabulary

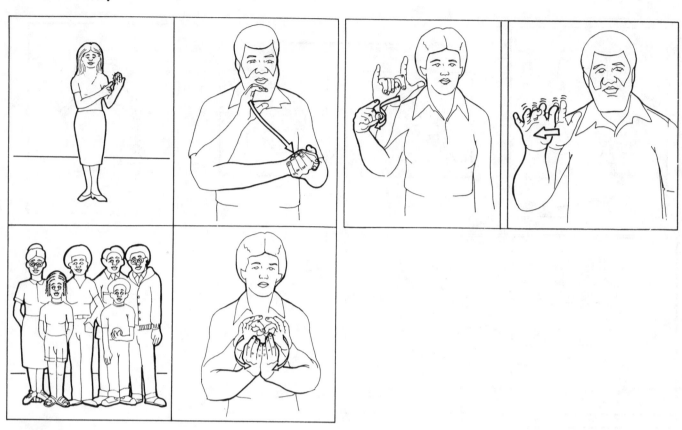

Definitions

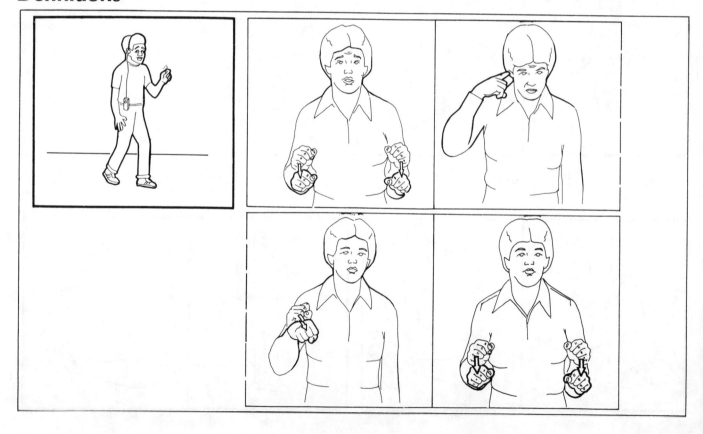

Definitions (continued)

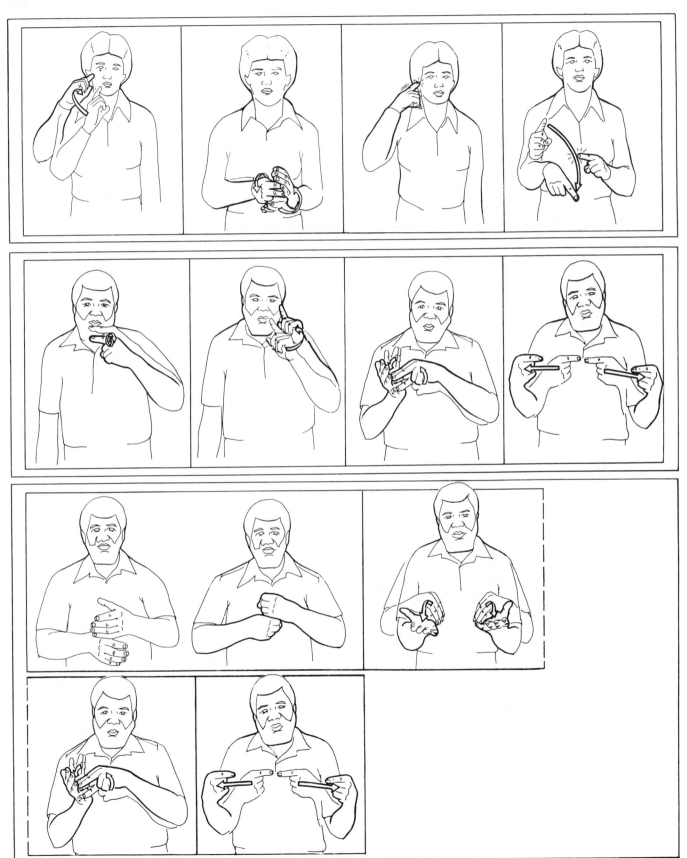

Classifiers and Pluralization

The classifier

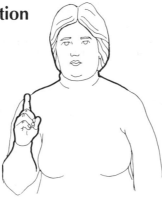

can be pluralized by incorporating numbers into it. For example:

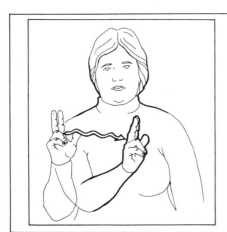

Numbers up to five can be used with this classifier. For different groupings, the handshape is changed.

Example 1

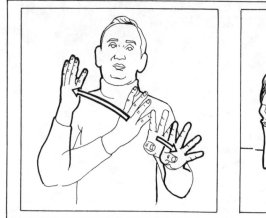 

Example 2

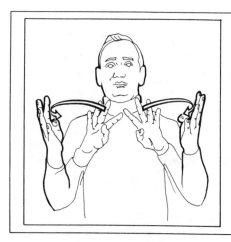 

Example 3

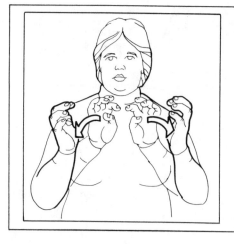 

Notice the difference in handshape between examples number 2 and 3.

Example 4

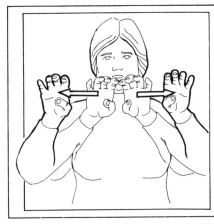 

Example 5

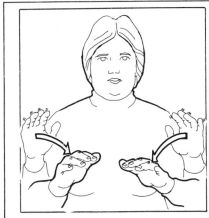 

Example 6

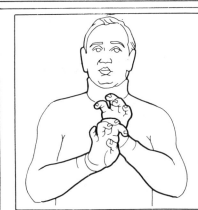 

Using these plural classifiers allows signers to pluralize nouns, much as they can be pluralized by adding definite or indefinite numbers to them.

Using the pictures below, show the numbers of people, animals or things in each using classifiers from this and previous lessons.

Incorporation of Number

In Lesson 9 you learned how numbers can be incorporated into time signs. They can also be incorporated when referring to age.

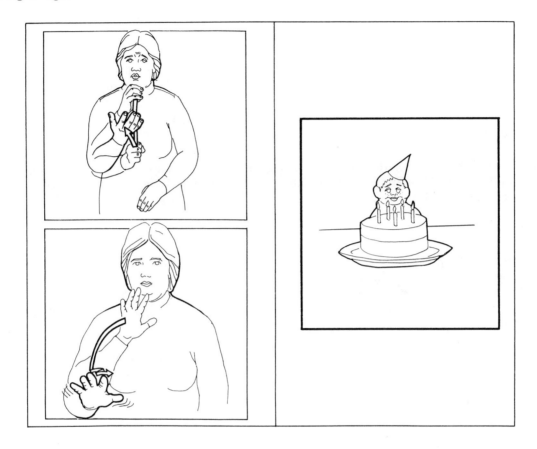

CULTURE

Captioned Films

The Division of Media Services in the Bureau of Education for the Handicapped provides captioned films free of charge to any group that has at least one Deaf person in it. This service was established in 1958, in the hope that Deaf people would be able to share equally with hearing people the artistic and cultural experience of films. Churches with Deaf congregations often have a regular evening when they show captioned films; sometimes a group of Deaf people will order films and regularly get together and watch the films.

With the invention of the telecaption decoder and the beginning of closed captioning on television, Deaf people have now begun to share in the artistic and cultural experience of television, which may have an effect on the popularity of captioned films, as well as other aspects of Deaf culture.

Interpreters

In 1964 the Registry of Interpreters for the Deaf was established. It is a national organization whose membership includes Deaf and hearing people and whose goals include upgrading the interpreting skills of its members, encouraging the training of new interpreters, educating the hearing public about deafness and interpreting, and providing a standard of interpreting services. To further these goals, in 1972 RID began evaluating its members who wished to be evaluated and certifying those who passed the evaluation.

Most states have chapters of RID which have regular meetings, hold workshops, and publish newsletters. For more information, write to the national office at: Registry of Interpreters for the Deaf, Inc., 814 Thayer Avenue, Silver Spring, Maryland 20910.

Residential Schools

Most states have residential schools for Deaf children, where the students live during the week, going home only for weekends and holidays. In the past, these schools were an important factor in the transmission of Deaf culture from one generation to another. Deaf children of Deaf parents, who learn ASL as their native language, are often the source for deaf children of hearing parents in learning ASL. In addition, residential schools often had Deaf adults who worked as dorm counselors or "house parents", and who, along with transmitting language and culture, also acted as role models for the Deaf children at the school. Many close bonds were formed in the residential schools, bonds that continued for the rest of the students' lives.

Gradually day schools for deaf children have also been developed. Students who attend these schools live at home and commute to school. Now there are day programs in the public schools in many large cities. While some of these programs hold classes separately from the hearing children in the school, in others the Deaf students are "mainstreamed" or integrated with the hearing students for all or some of their classes. With the passage by Congress in 1975 of the Education for All Handicapped Children Act (P.L. 94-142), which requires states to give to all handicapped children a free and "appropriate" education, greater emphasis has been placed on mainstreaming.

Vocabulary

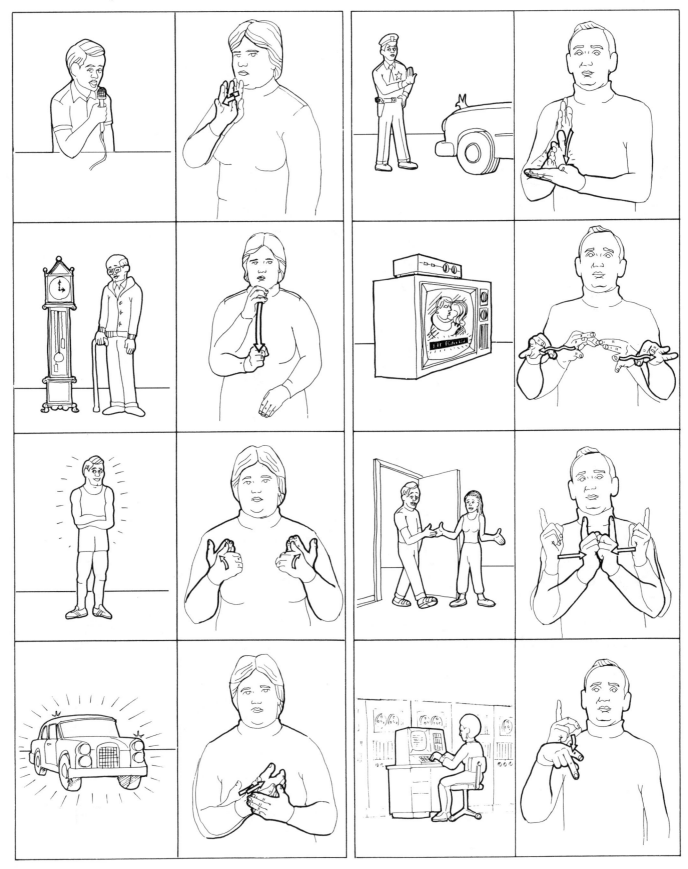

Definitions

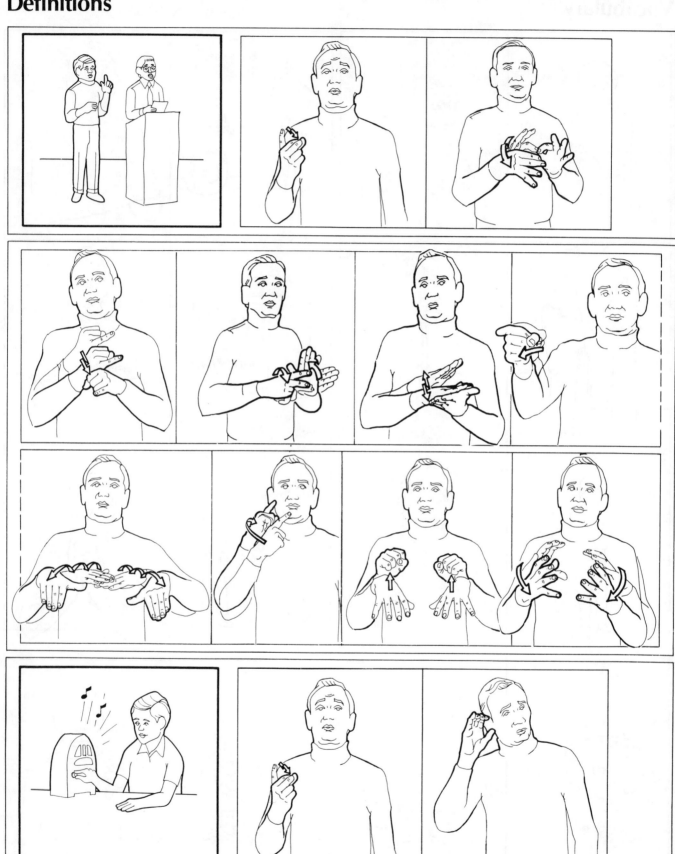

Definitions (continued)

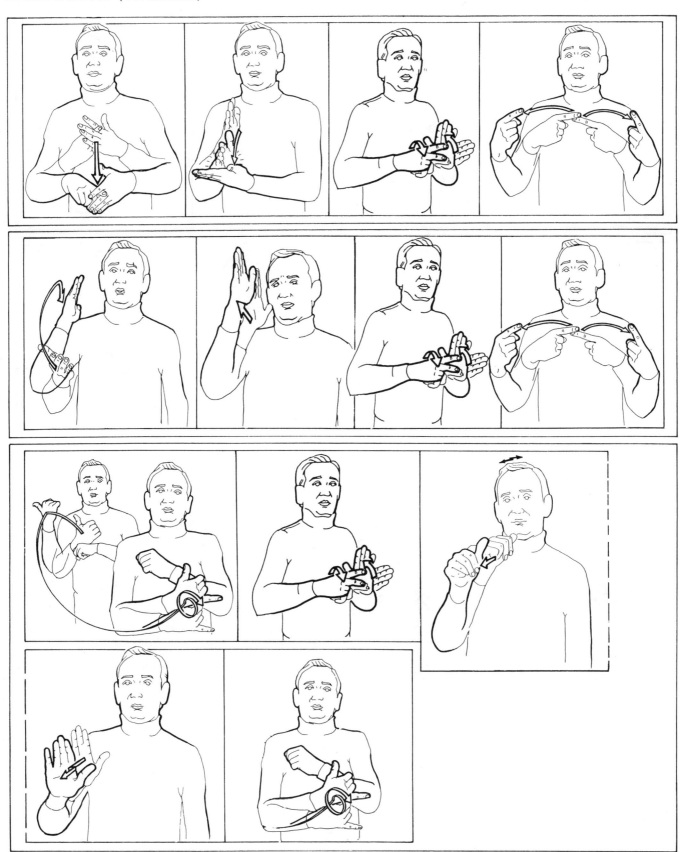

Definitions (continued)

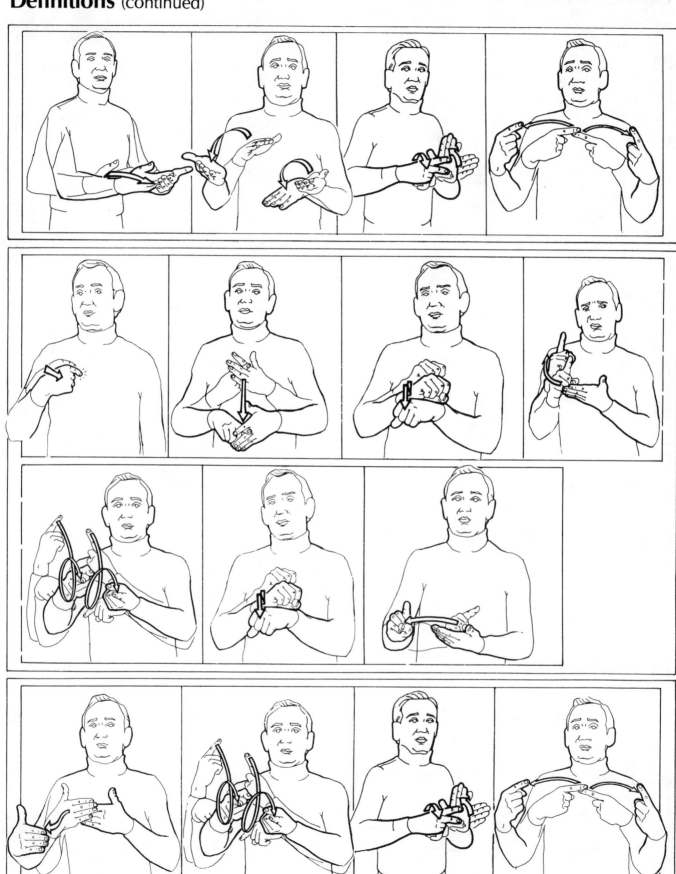

Inflection of Verbs: Distributional Aspect

Lesson 4 introduced directional verbs and some ways they could be moved to show the relation between the subject(s) and object(s) of a sentence. They also can be inflected to show the distribution of an action, meaning how many people are involved in receiving the action. For example:

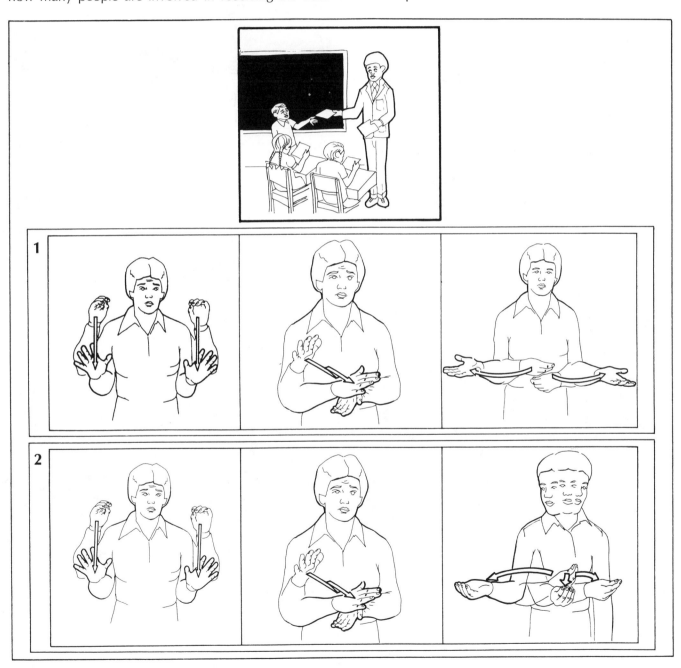

In both sentences the verb is inflected to show the action in the picture above. In sentence 1, the group is seen as a whole and the action as a one-time event. In sentence 2, the focus is on individuals and the action is seen as happening to each one of them separately.

The direction in which the sign is made will vary if the signer is talking about something done to a third party

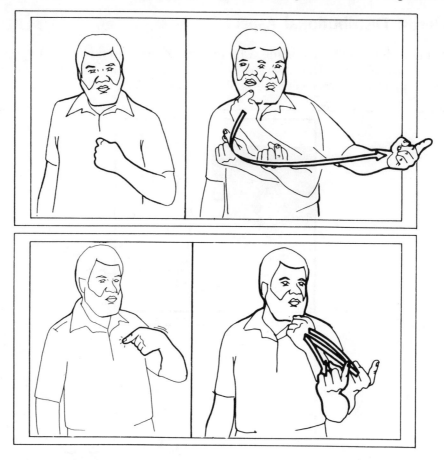

or to the addressee. (In this example and the addressee is plural).

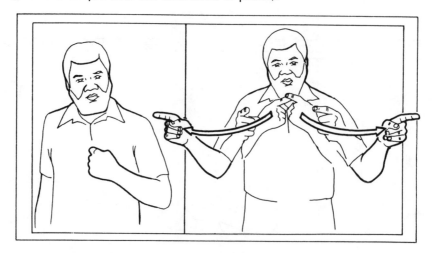

Here are some more verbs that can be inflected in this way:

Fingerspelled Loan Words

One way languages have of expanding their vocabulary is to borrow words from other languages. In the process, the foreign words take on the pronunciation and follow the grammatical rules of the language which has borrowed them. English has many borrowed words, and ASL has a number of signs that were borrowed from English. These signs were originally fingerspelled as one would fingerspell any English word, but gradually they were influenced by ASL and took on the characteristics of signs. Now they are not English words at all, but ASL signs. Fingerspelled loan words occurred in Lessons 4 and 8; another is:

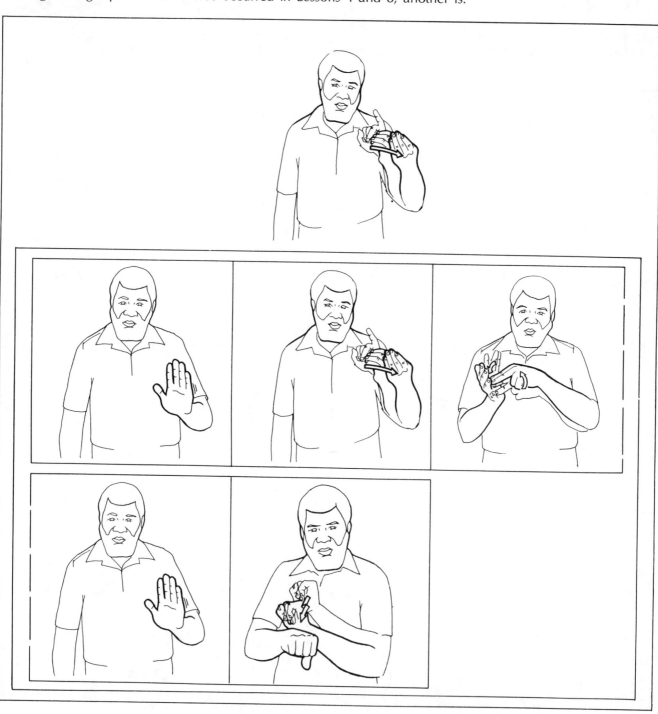

Deaf Education in America

The first successful school for Deaf people in America was established in Hartford, Connecticut, in 1817 by Laurent Clerc and Thomas Hopkins Gallaudet. Gallaudet, an American, had gone to Europe to learn methods for teaching deaf children at the request of his neighbor, Dr. Mason Cogswell, whose daughter Alice was deaf. Gallaudet went first to England where he hoped to learn the methods developed by Thomas Braidwood during the 18th century and continued by his family in England and Scotland after his death. The methods the Braidwoods used were oral, emphasizing speech, reading and writing and strongly discouraging any use of signs. However, the directors of the schools in England and Scotland all refused to divulge their methods. Fortunately, at the same time Gallaudet was in London, he attended a lecture given by three men from France, l'Abbé Sicard, Laurent Clerc and Jean Massieu. Clerc and Massieu were both deaf, had been students at the Paris school, and later became teachers. Along with Sicard, they would travel about, giving lectures and demonstrations of their methods, which used signs from French Sign Language, and additional signs developed by the founder of the Paris school, l'Abbé Michel de l'Epeé, to help French Deaf students learn written French. When Gallaudet approached the three men and explained his purpose, they invited him to come to France and study with them. He did, and several months later returned to America with Clerc, whom he had persuaded to join him, and together they established the school at Hartford.

Although Clerc and Gallaudet brought the sign language used at the Paris school to America, the Deaf people living there at the time had signs of their own. There were in fact probably as many different varieties of signed languages as there were isolated groups of Deaf people. The establishment of the school at Hartford, however, gave Deaf people from all over the country the opportunity to gather in one place, and from the roots of their various languages (old American Sign Language), combined with that used by Clerc and Gallaudet, grew present day American Sign Language.

Oralism and Manualism

Ever since the field of deaf education began, people have been divided over the best methods to use. Teachers, most of them hearing, have argued endlessly over the merits of oral vs. manual teaching methods. The very first school for Deaf people in America was an oral school, Cobb's school in Virginia. It only lasted a short time however, and when the Hartford school was begun in 1817, the use of signs to teach deaf people was introduced in America. Later, people trained by Clerc went on to establish schools for Deaf people in other states, continuing the manual methods brought from France by Gallaudet and Clerc.

Gradually, however, there came to be an increasing demand for oral training. One of the strongest proponents of oralism was Alexander Graham Bell, who felt that if Deaf people were taught using sign language, they would never learn to speak or lipread and thus never be able to function effectively in a hearing world. Many hearing parents of children who were deaf (and most deaf children have hearing parents) also supported an oralist approach, and schools that used only oral methods were established. Eventually even state residential schools began using oral methods. Deaf teachers were no longer hired and oralism became the preferred mode of instruction.

In time, of course, things began to swing back the other way. In the late 1960's and early 1970's a new theory in deaf education was proposed: total communication. As a teaching philosophy, it states that all means practicable to teach Deaf children should be used—signs, reading, writing, lipreading, speech training, and hearing aids to augment any residual hearing a child might have. At the same time, some teachers developed several systems to code English into signs. Although people were beginning to accept the idea that Deaf children could learn more easily through a visual than an auditory mode, ASL was not the language they wished to use to teach them. Indeed, at the time that total communication came to the forefront of deaf education, ASL was not widely recognized as a language. It was thought instead to be bad or ungrammatical English. Thus, teachers wanted a method to code an auditory/vocal language—English—into a visual mode. Several systems of manually coded English (M.C.E.) were developed and are now being used to teach Deaf children.

And now that the majority of schools and programs for deaf youngsters use some form of manual communication, a new controversy is brewing. Many teachers of deaf children seem to strongly believe that teaching English is of primary importance, and would consider the use of ASL in the classroom to be detrimental to the students' learning of English. Some members of the Deaf Community, however, feel that to deprive Deaf children of ASL is to deprive them of part of their heritage and culture. And, as there is no proof that M.C.E. is an effective tool for teaching English, some people are beginning to wonder why ASL cannot also be used for that purpose. They feel that Deaf children should have the opportunity to be bilingual, that English has its place, but that ASL has at the very least an equal place in the classroom.

Post-Secondary Education for Deaf Students

Gallaudet College was for a long time the only institution of higher learning available for Deaf students. It began as a private school in Washington, D.C. in 1856, founded by Amos Kendall, with Edward Miner Gallaudet (Thomas' son) as its director. In 1864, it was refounded by Congress, becoming Columbia Institution, and in 1894 changed its name to Gallaudet College, in honor of Thomas Hopkins Gallaudet. The preparatory department was named Kendall School, after the original founder.

In 1964, California State University at Northridge began making its programs available to Deaf students. Eventually programs were also established in various community colleges around the nation. Now, under Section 504 of the Rehabilitation Act of 1973, all programs and facilities receiving federal funds must provide equal access to all handicapped students, which in theory should enable a Deaf student to attend any public college and many private ones.

For Deaf students wishing to pursue technical careers there is the National Technical Institute for the Deaf, located on the campus of the Rochester Institute of Technology in Rochester, New York. It opened in 1968 and was established to give Deaf people the opportunity for post secondary education in technical fields.

Vocabulary

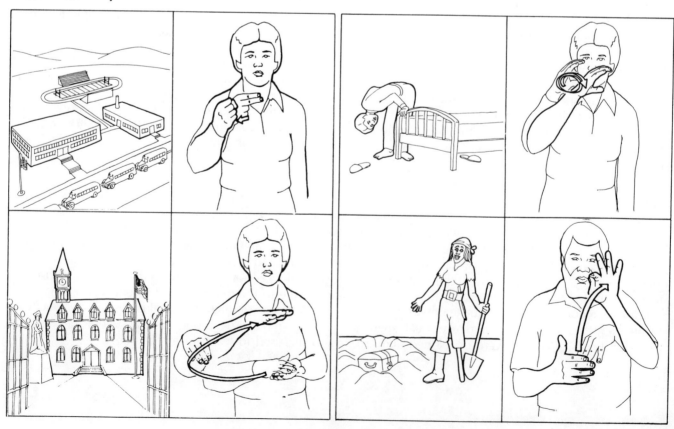

Vocabulary (continued)

Definitions

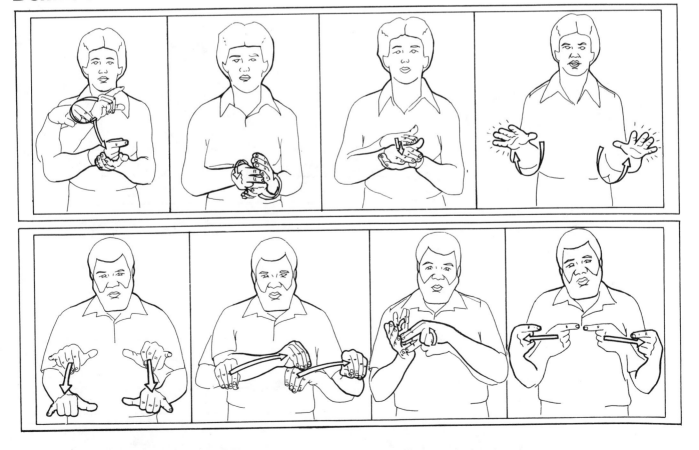

Definitions (continued)

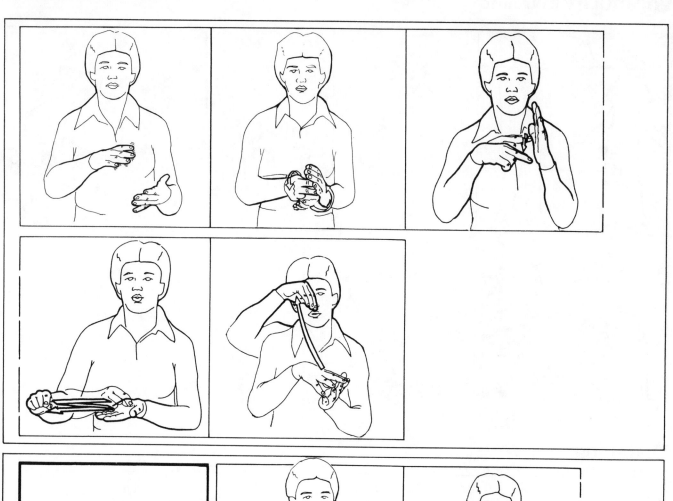

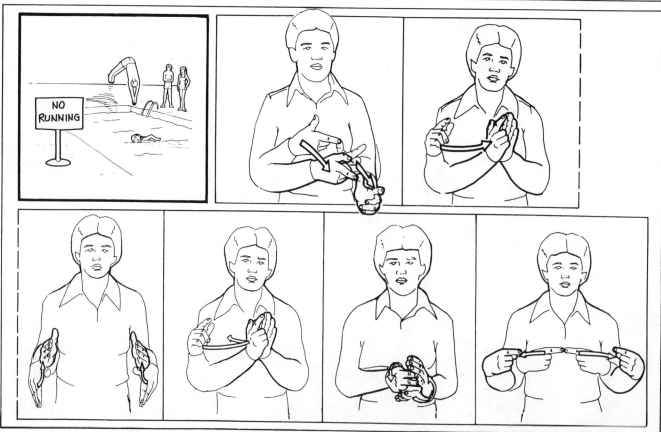

Definitions (continued)

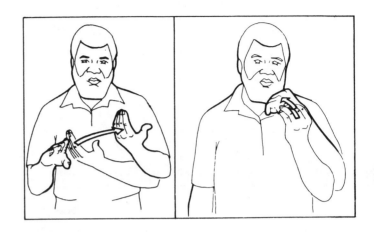

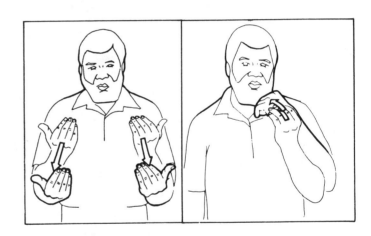

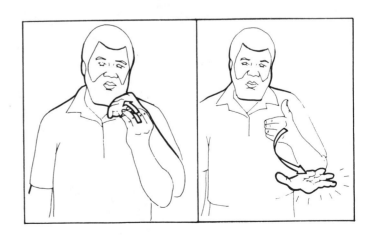

Definitions (continued)

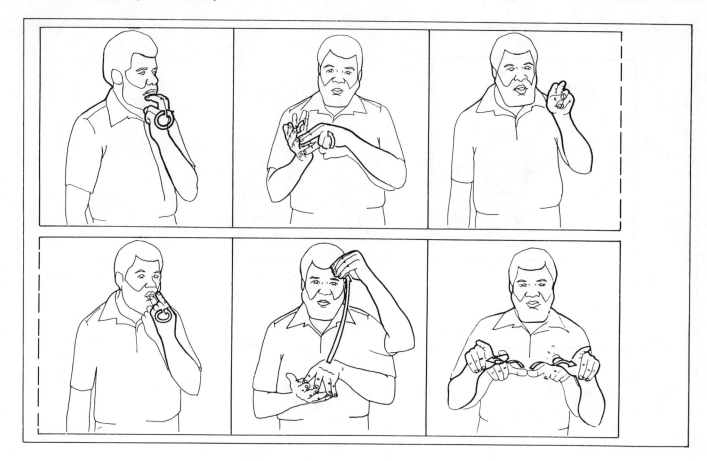

Definitions (continued)

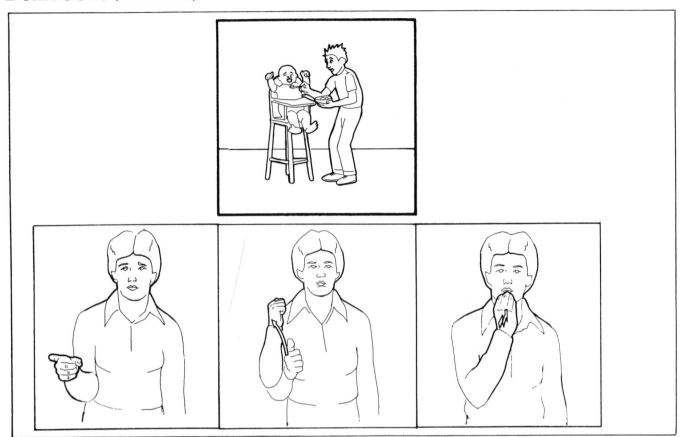

Even More Classifiers

Classifiers Functioning as Verbs

Lesson 15 introduced plural classifiers for large numbers of things (pp. 148-149). Like other classifiers, these can function as verbs if movement is added to them. For example:

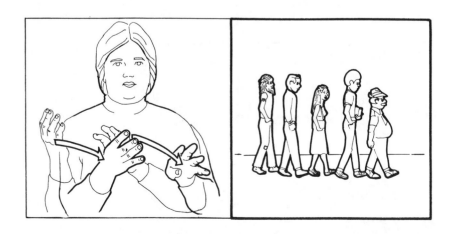

Pluralization of Singular Classifiers

Singular classifiers can be pluralized by repeating them, a process somewhat similar to pluralizing nouns by repeating them. For example:

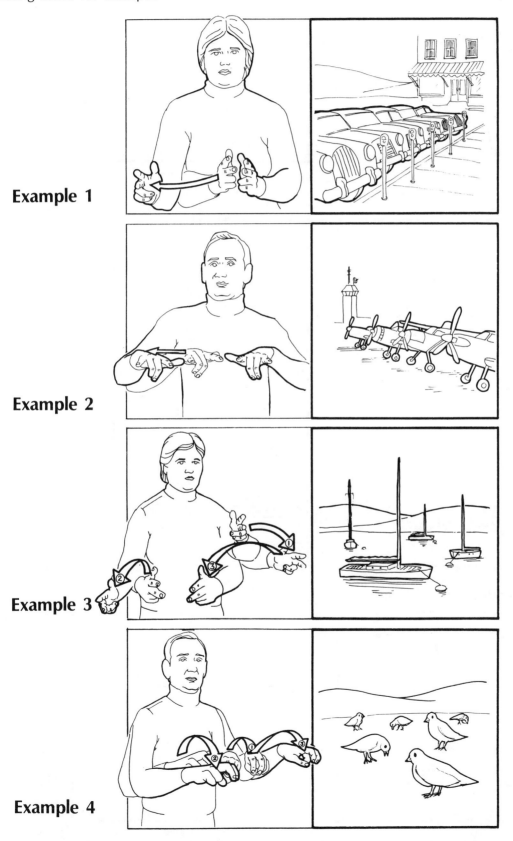

Example 1

Example 2

Example 3

Example 4

In Examples 1 & 2 on the previous page, notice how the signer's non-dominant hand remained in place. This technique is used again in Examples 5 and 6 below and helps establish the relation of the things to one another.

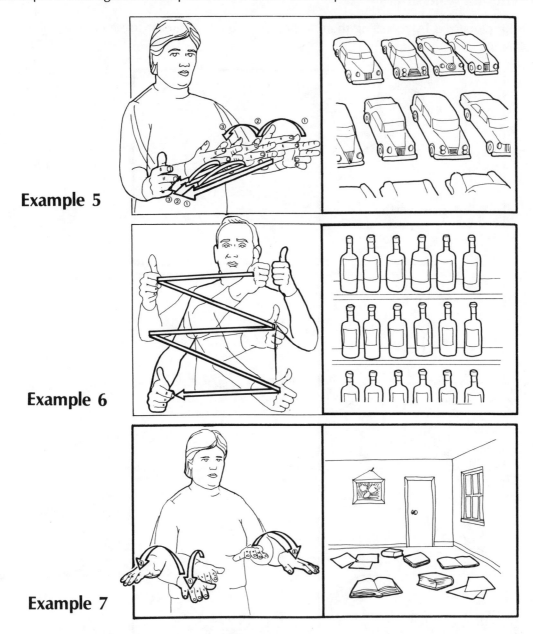

Example 5

Example 6

Example 7

Describe the pictures below using classifiers.

Incorporating Numbers: Time

In Lesson 9 you saw how numbers can be incorporated into signs referring to units of time, and in Lesson 15 how numbers are incorporated into a sign relating to age. Here is another way numbers are incorporated into signs for time:

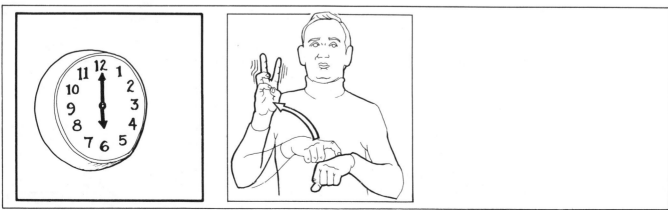

Vocabulary

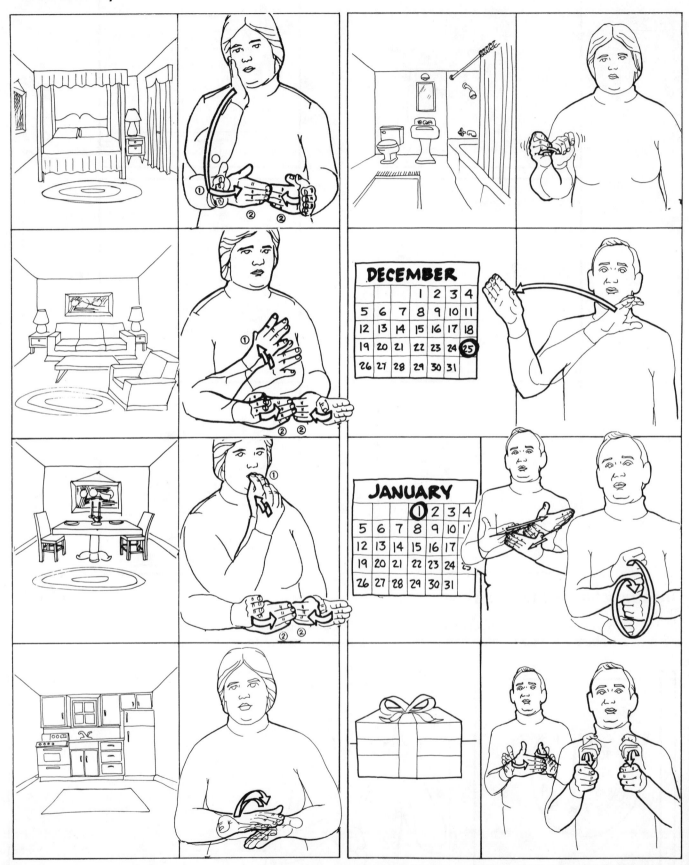

Vocabulary (continued)

Definitions

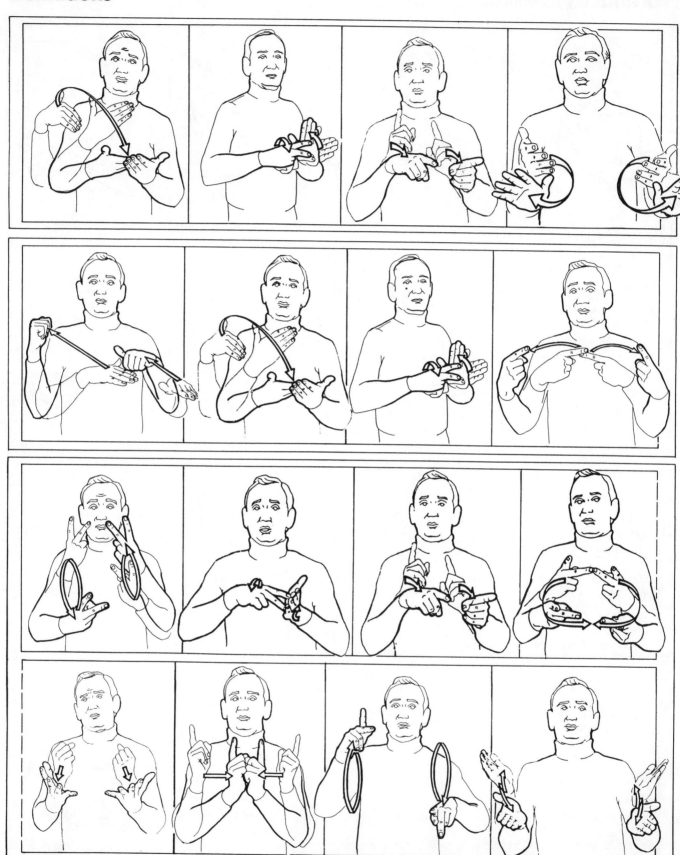

Definitions (continued)

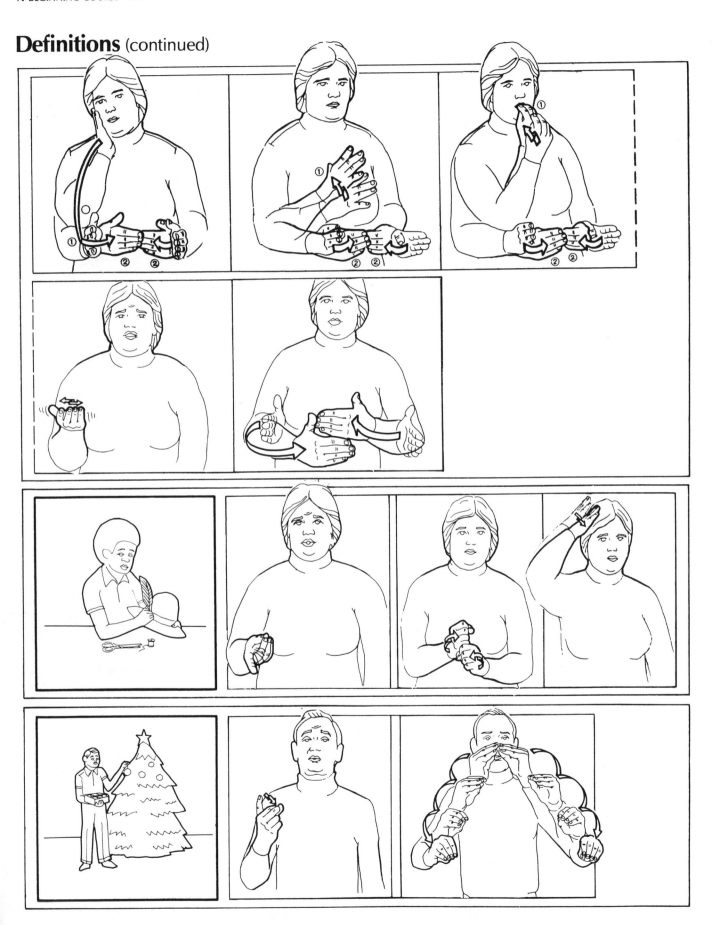

Modifying Adjectives

Here are some more examples of adjectives made more intense by the non-manual grammatical signal intoduced in Lesson 4, and later used with some adjectives in Lesson 11 (p. 102 & 103):

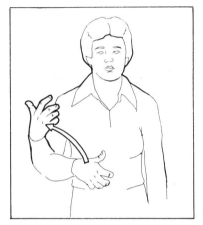 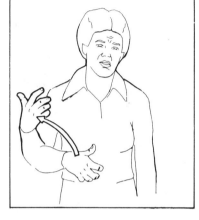

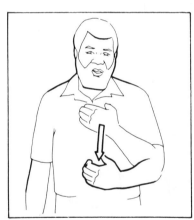 

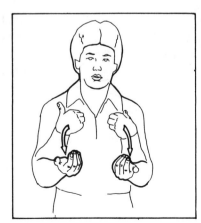 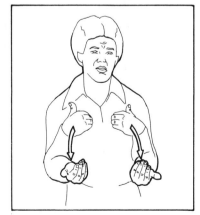

The signer's attitude about a situation can influence the degree to which the signal is used, that is, how intensely the intense signal is made.

Pronominalization: Direct Address

Another form of pronominalization in ASL occurs when the signer uses a shift in body position and eye gaze to index characters in a story. In effect, the signer becomes the different characters, often taking on some of their physical characteristics and attitudes. For example:

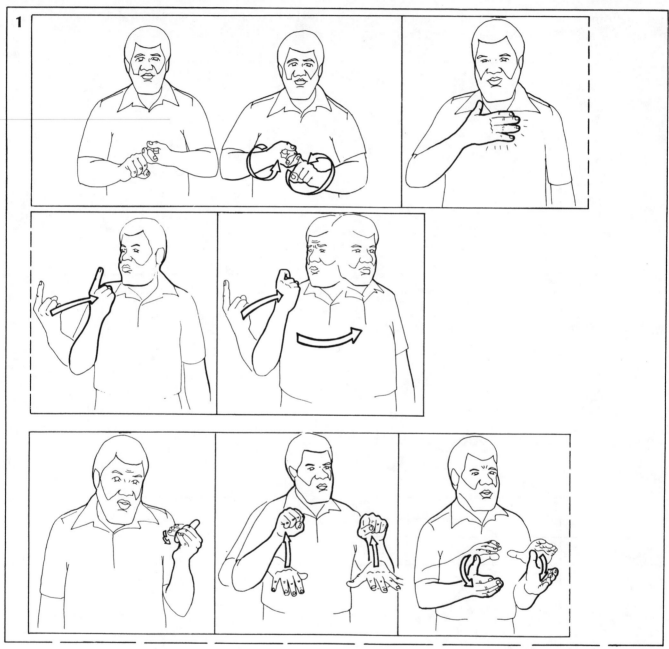

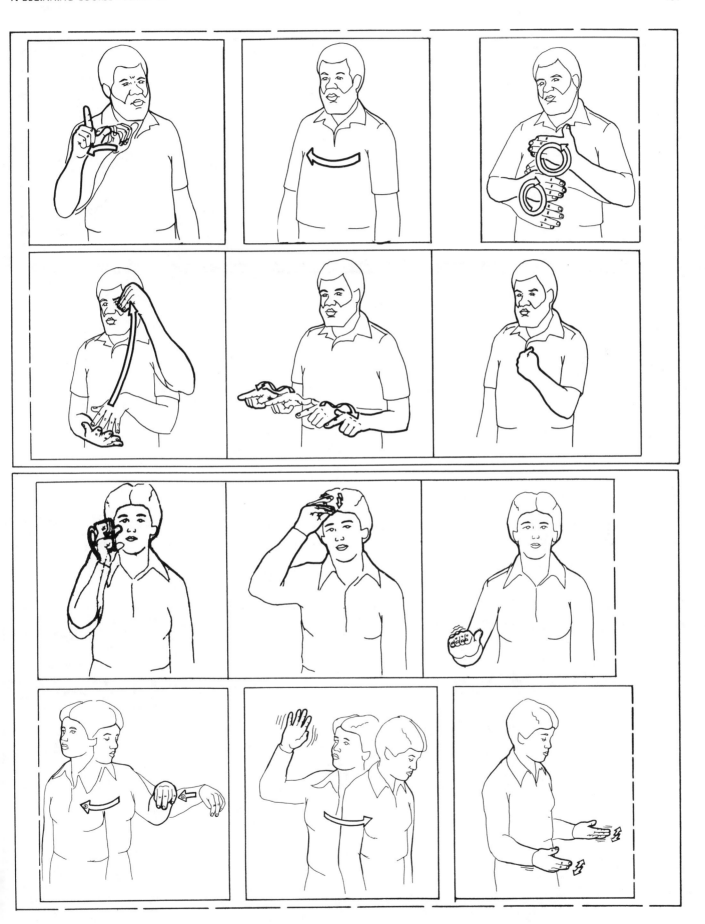

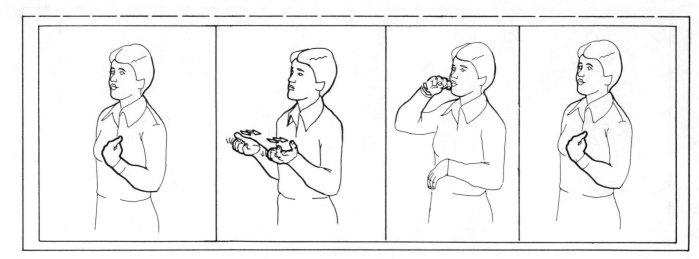

Notice how the signer's gaze is downward for the adult speaking to the child, and up for the child speaking to the adult.

Vocabulary

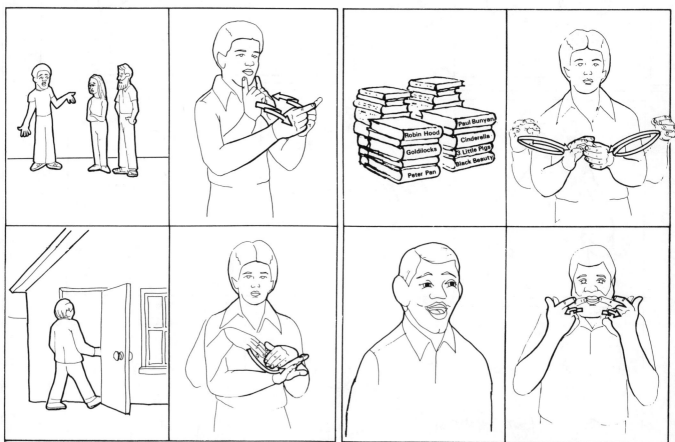

Vocabulary (continued)

Vocabulary (continued)

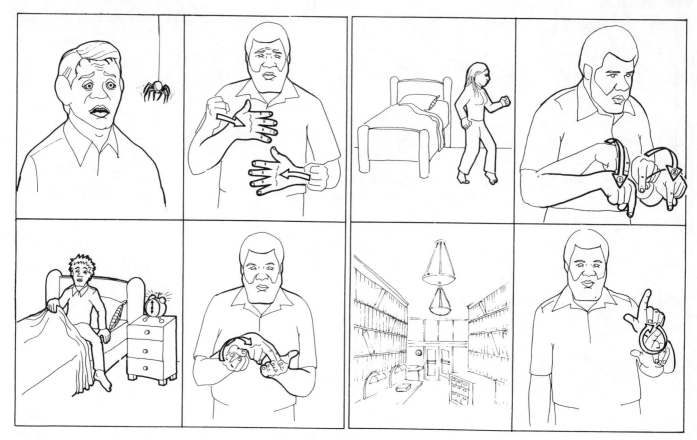

Definitions

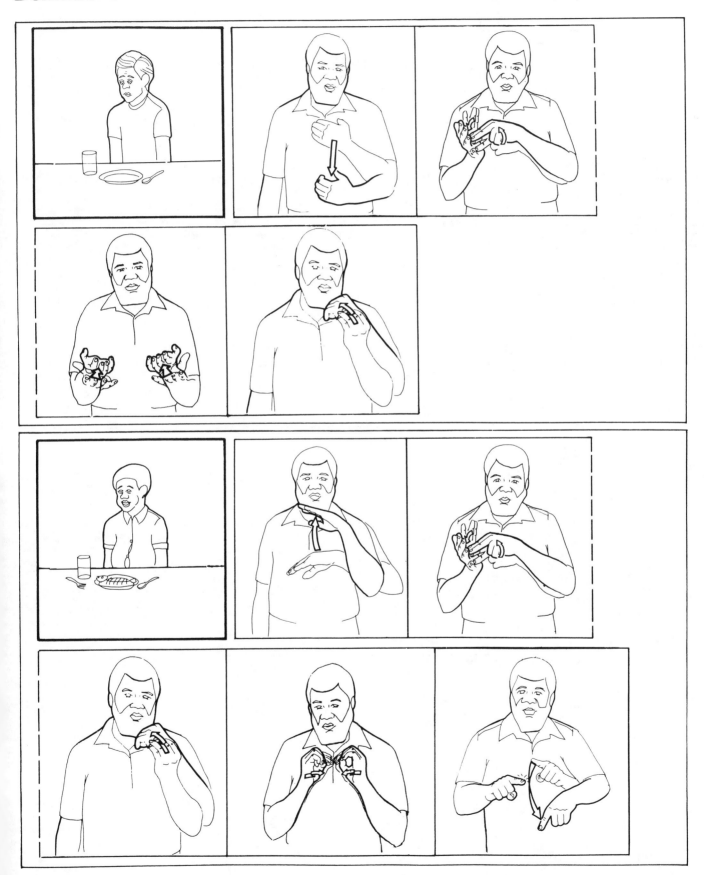

Definitions (continued)

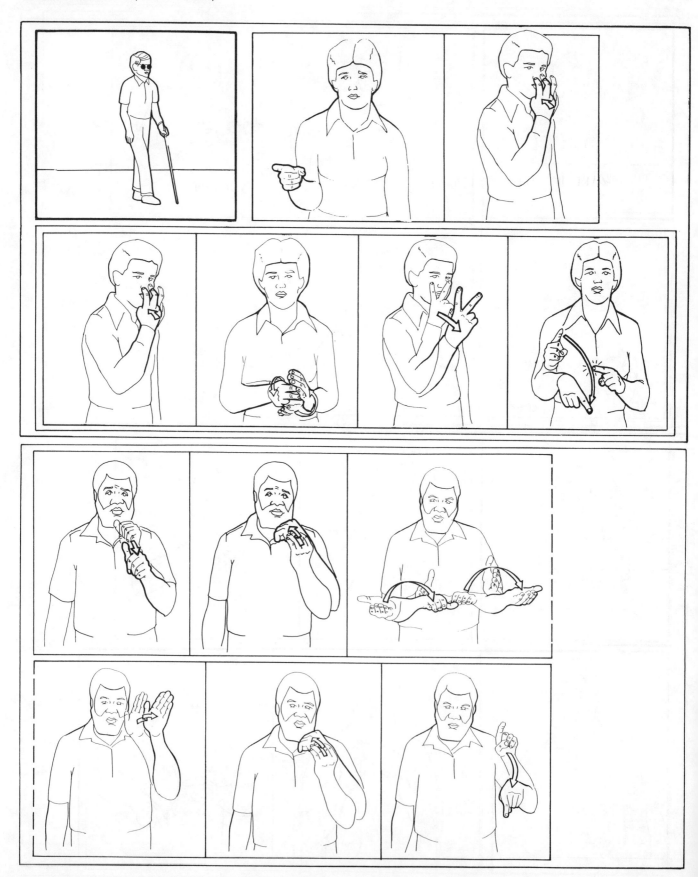

Vocabulary (continued)

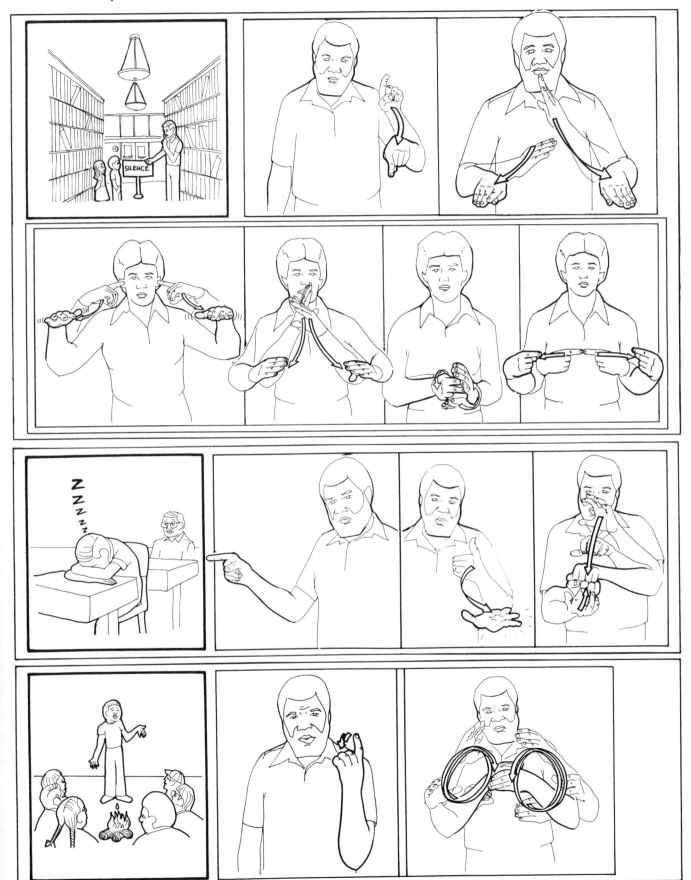

Inflection of Adjectives: Regularly and Continually

Lesson 9 (p. 83) first introduced an inflection that could be used with many action verbs, and which showed that the action was done repeatedly or on a regular basis. This same inflection can be used with some adjectives. For example:

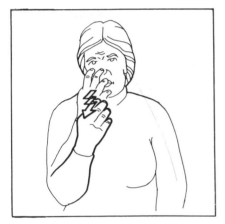

Lesson 12 (p. 111) introduced another inflection which showed that action was done continually. This inflection also can be used with some adjectives.

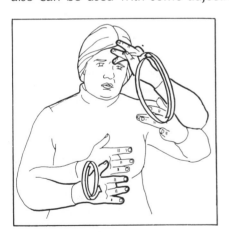
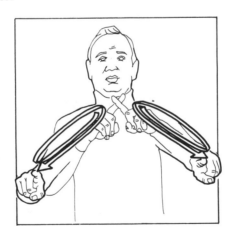
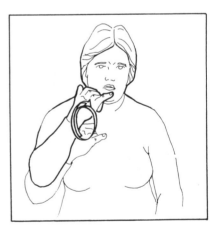

Inflection of Adjectives: Change of State

In ASL, adjectives can be inflected to show a person changing from one state to the state shown by the adjective. For example:

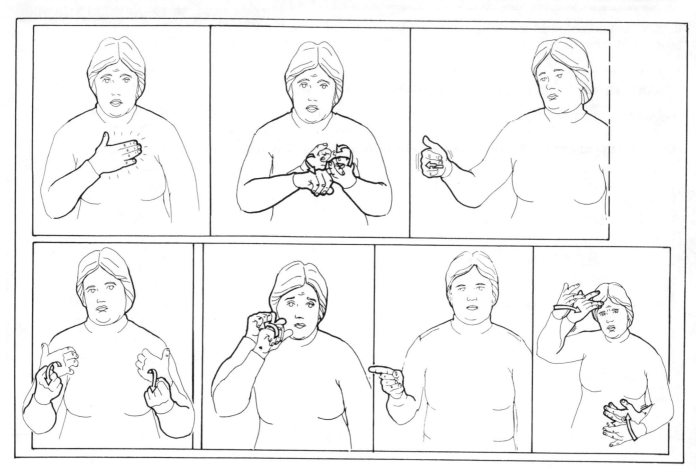

CULTURE

Causes of Deafness

There are several causes of deafness, some occurring before birth or shortly thereafter, and some occurring later in a person's life.

Genetic factors account for 50-60% of all deafness. The other major cause of pre-natal deafness is rubella, which often causes other complications with the heart, eyes, brain and skeletal system. Except during epidemics (the last of which was from 1963-1965), rubella accounts for only about 10% of pre-natal deafness.

Blood type incompatibility or premature birth can both be causes of deafness shortly after birth. In later childhood, meningitis (an inflammation of the membranes surrounding the brain and spinal cord) or encephalitis can cause deafness. Encephalitis can occur if the child has a virus disease such as measles or mumps and the virus migrates and infects the brain. Blows to the head, damage to the auditory nerve or ear drum, and loud noises, especially over a prolonged period of time, can all cause deafness. In addition, certain medications, given to save people's lives, may leave them with a degenerative hearing loss.

TTYs

A TTY is a teletypewriter, a device that can be coupled to a telephone and which has a typewriter-like keyboard onto which messages are typed. The old style TTYs were large machines with a roll of paper on which the message appeared. New models, developed in the last few years, are portable, generally have an electronic display, and do not need special coupling equipment. Some newer models also have a paper roll or have an attachment which allows the message to be printed as well as displayed electronically.

To communicate via TTY each party must have one; so far no one has produced a machine that will decode the human voice into electronic impulses for a TTY and the TTY signal into a human voice. As the general public becomes more aware of deafness, more and more businesses are purchasing TTYs, as well as federal, state, and local government agencies.

When receiving a TTY call, you must type out both a greeting and your name, as TTY typing is generally anonymous, and a simple "hello" could leave the caller wondering who is on the other end of the line. The letters GA (go ahead) are used at the end of a block of conversation to let the other party know that it is all right for them to proceed. At the end of the communication one party will type a farewell, and then GA TO SK, indicating that their half of the conversation is concluded. When the other party is also finished, they will type SKSK.

The telephone is usually connected to a signalling device which in turn can have a lamp plugged into it. When the phone rings, the light flashes, alerting whoever is there. Lights are also used as signalling devices for doorbells, alarm clocks and to monitor a baby's cries.

Vocabulary

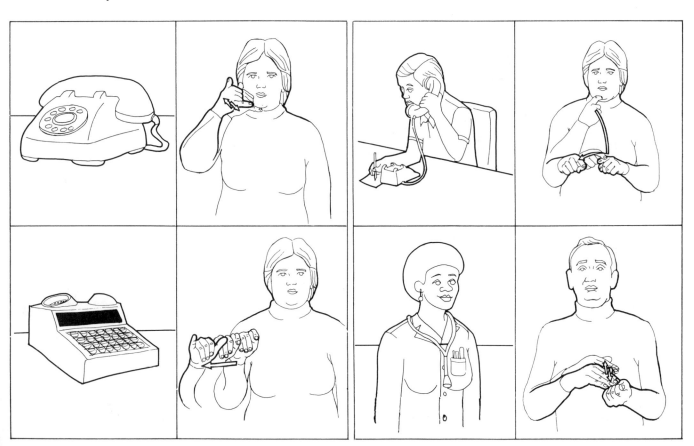

Vocabulary (continued)

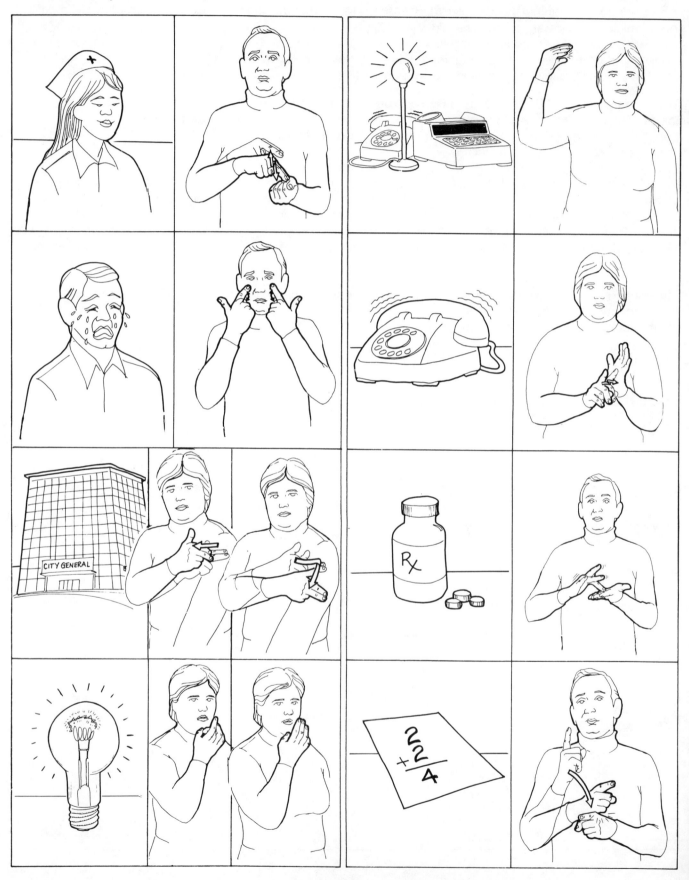

Vocabulary (continued)

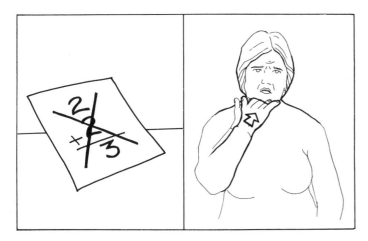

Definitions

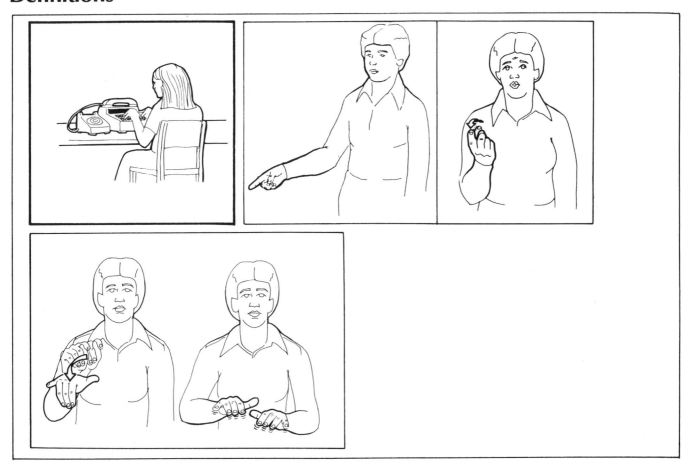

Definitions (continued)

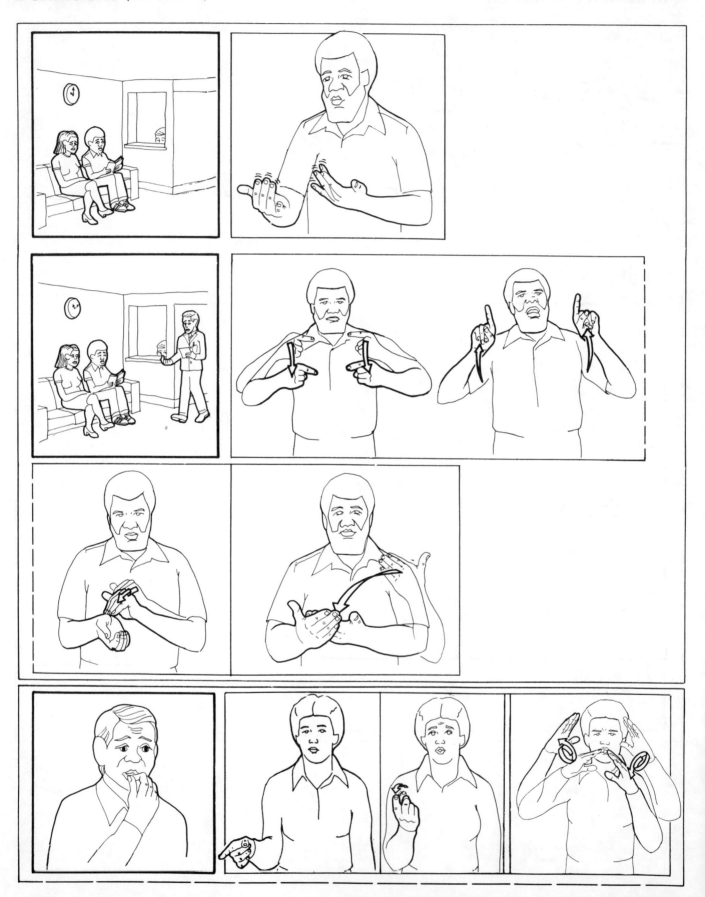

Definitions (continued)

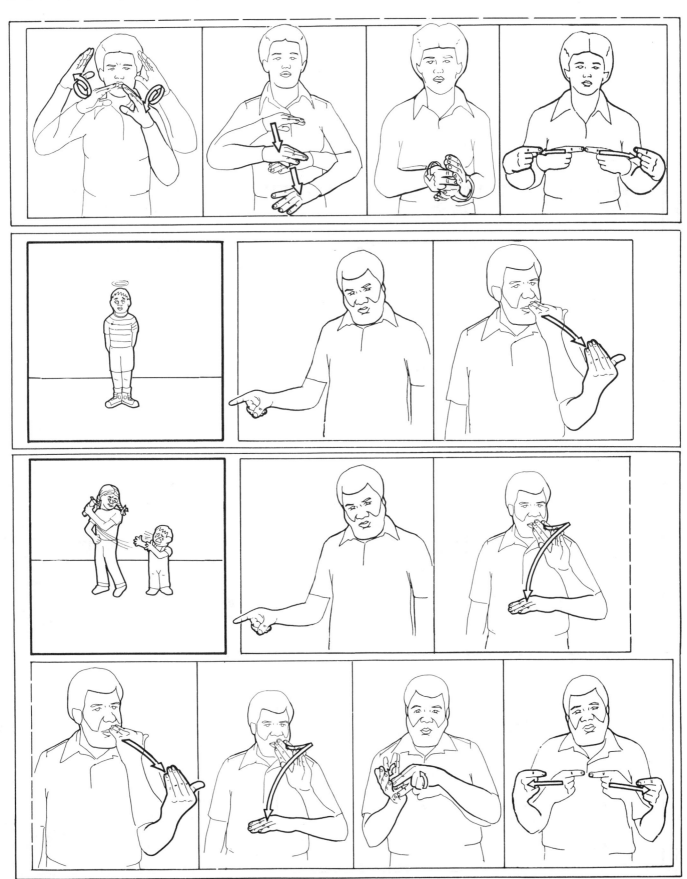

Definitions (continued)

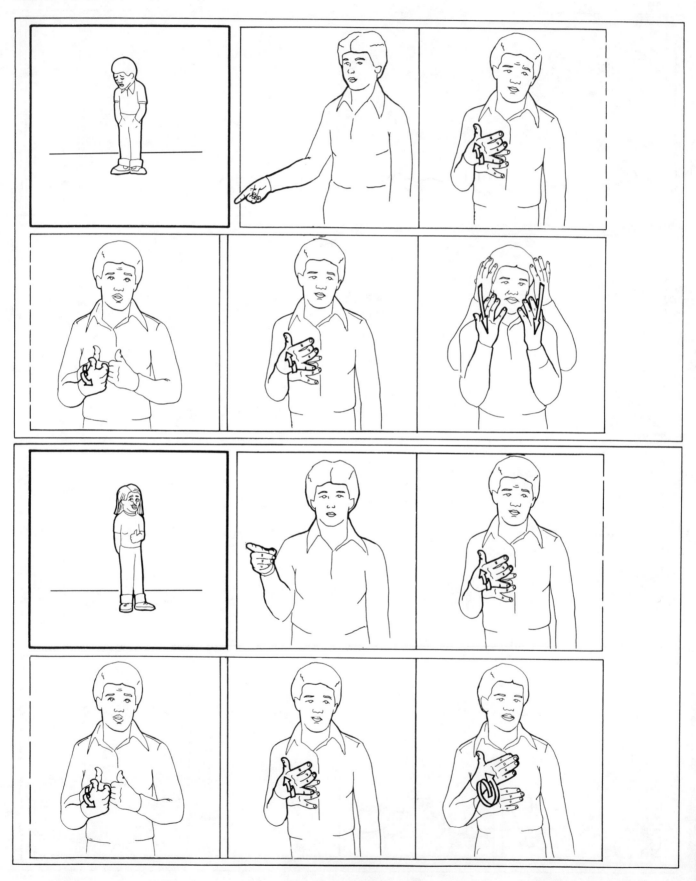

Definitions (continued)

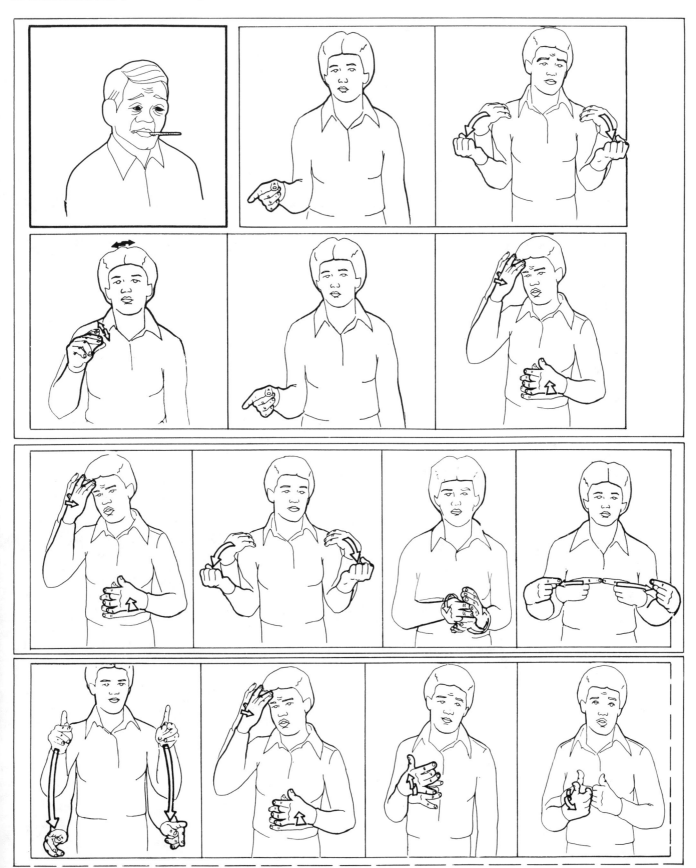

Definitions (continued)

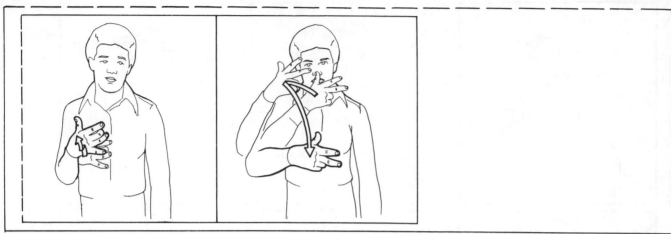

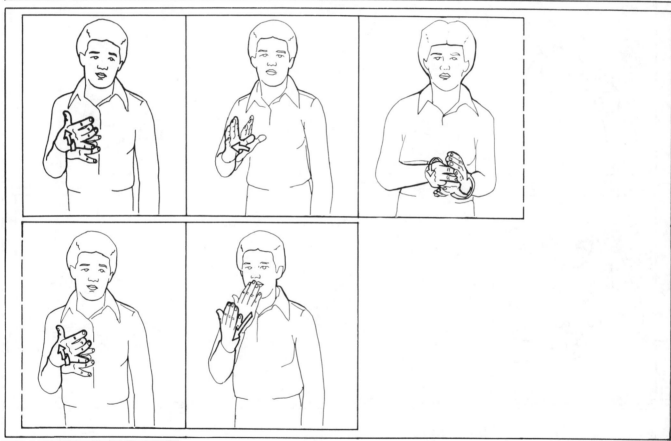

Index